Praise for *Sweater Quest*

"I could NOT put *Sweater Quest* down! I felt as though I was knitting the sweater along with Adrienne, felt her pain and her joy. Once I even thought, as I was packing the car, 'Now WHERE is that Alice Starmore sweater I was working on?' The book became *that* insinuated into my psyche. I love this book."

—Annie Modesitt, author of *Confessions of a Knitting Heretic*

"This is a delicious, delicious book. *Sweater Quest* is an epic, funny travelogue—a sort of *Borat,* except with yarn. (And no Kazakh accent.) This is the story of a sweater, but at its heart this is the story of a knitter who may have bitten off more than she can chew—and therein lies the tale. Adrienne's travels down the rabbit hole of the knitting world make this story absolutely perfect for everyone who understands that there is no such thing as too much knitting. Every knitter will identify with Adrienne Martini's all-in obsession. Put down your needles for a few minutes and come along for a wild, wild ride."

—Ann Shayne, coauthor with Kay Gardiner of *Mason-Dixon Knitting*

"What a delightful book! Adrienne Martini's witty, breezy account of her beyond-admirable knitting project is sure to please."

—Maggie Sefton, *New York Times* bestselling author of the Kelly Flynn Knitting Mysteries

"I love this odyssey, and Adrienne's writing. I am so glad she is willing to share it with any reader (knitter or not) who is attracted to an improbable, obsessive journey."

—Linda Roghaar, coeditor with Molly Wolf of *KnitLit, KnitLit (too),* and *KnitLit the Third*

Also by Adrienne Martini

Hillbilly Gothic

Sweater Quest

My Year of Knitting Dangerously

Adrienne Martini

Free Press

New York London Toronto Sydney

Free Press
A Division of Simon & Schuster, Inc.
1230 Avenue of the Americas
New York, NY 10020

First Free Press trade paperback edition March 2010

FREE PRESS and colophon are trademarks of Simon & Schuster, Inc.

Designed by Carla Jayne Jones

Manufactured in the United States of America

10 9 8 7 6 5 4 3 2 1

Library of Congress Cataloging-in-Publication Data
Martini, Adrienne.
Sweater quest : my year of knitting dangerously / Adrienne Martini.
p. cm.
1. Knitting. 2. Sweaters—Scotland—Fair Isle. 3. Knitters (Persons)
4. Martini, Adrienne, 1971– I. Title.
TT825.M27595 2010
746.43'20922—dc22
2009031901

ISBN 978-1-4165-9764-3
ISBN 978-1-4165-9766-7 (ebook)

For Cory, because his sister got the first one

Contents

Introduction

I knit so I don't kill people.

—bumper sticker spotted at Rhinebeck Sheep and Wool Festival

Had I not discovered knitting, I would not be the paragon of sanity that I am today.

No, really.

When I had my first baby in 2002, I lost my mind. And by "lost my mind," I don't intend to imply minor weepiness or fleeting unhappiness. Two weeks into my maternity leave, I checked myself into my local psych ward because I'd become a danger to myself. At the time, it seemed that reclaiming even a shred of my former aplomb would be impossible. Now the whole event feels like it happened to someone else.

Time is a great balm, of course. So are high-grade pharmaceuticals. But what really helped turn the tide was knitting. Now most of the drugs are a distant memory. The yarn, however, is still with me. So are baskets of knitted hats, scarves, sweaters, and socks.

With some input from my husband, I also made a second kid. That, however, is a story that differs little from what we were all taught in health class. My body used the pattern it is encoded with and knitted up a boy baby this time.

After my son's birth, nothing unexpected happened. My husband and I lost sleep. We wondered when we'd ever stop doing six loads of laundry every day. My older child did her best to adjust to the new blob who, she believed, supplanted her in her parents' affections. We did our best to assure her that she was loved.

Occasionally I did burst into tears, but I was able to stop again relatively quickly, which was a big change from the first time around. I also spent some of the mothering downtime, those moments when the wee one only wants to sleep in your lap, knitting a sweater for my very tall husband. It wasn't anything fancy, just miles and miles of garter stitch, which is an amazing tonic to frayed and exhausted nerves.

Had you asked me a decade ago what I'd see myself doing in the future, "obsessively knitting" would not have been in the Top Ten possible answers. Like so many women who were girls in the seventies, at some point I was taught to knit, which I promptly forgot in favor of swooning over Leif Garrett and perfecting my eye roll. I learned again shortly before getting pregnant the first time, when the most recent round of knitting mania swept through the United States. After all, if Julia Roberts can knit, so can I. That and a fondness for Lyle Lovett can be what we have in common.

I knitted a lot of hats during my first baby's first year, simply because hats are criminally easy to knit. Once you get the basics down, even if you are sleep deprived and leaking bodily fluids, a hat requires minimal mental gymnastics.

I could finish a hat in about a week, working on it when the baby was on my lap, which seemed like every waking moment of every endless day. Each finished hat made me feel that I had at least accomplished something short-term and tangible. From sticks and some string, I'd crafted a useful item. Given that the other project, who was cooing in my lap, was definitely a long-term action item, these little hats made me feel as if I could still finish what I'd started as long as I kept my projects small.

Like a baby, knitting is a gift that keeps surprising you. Baby surprises tend to be immediate and bipolar—either "that's cool!" or "that's disgusting!"—but knitting surprises are subtle and enduring. Making stuff with my very own hands has enriched my life in innumerable ways. Both kids and craft have taught me how to deal with frustration so acute that I'd want to bite the head off a kitten. Both are great courses in expectation management. Both have given more than they've taken—and introduced me to a community that I otherwise never would have known.

Moms are different from nonmoms, which isn't to say that we can't understand women without children; it's just that women with kids (no matter how they wound up with them) can identify with other moms in a stronger way. That's not to say that we all endorse each other's choices (and if you ever want to start a hair-pulling fight, state an opinion on breastfeeding to a room full of moms) but that we bond with each other in an innate way.

Knitters immediately bond with other knitters too. Amy R. Singer states it best in her 2002 manifesto for Knitty.com: "We are different, aren't we? Knitters. We take strands of fiber and from them we create wonders. We share what we know. We're anxious to do it. We want there to be more of us. People who look at the world a little differently. A little less gimme and a little more let me try that. We enjoy process as much as product. We knit."

Which isn't to say that the knitting community is a monolithic entity in which all the members hold hands and sing "Kumbaya" on a regular basis. You can easily start another hair-pulling fight by stating an opinion on buttonholes. And if you want a real melee—seriously, the authorities would have to be called—mention your feelings about buttonholes having to be on the left side of a woman's garment while a knitter-mom is breastfeeding a six-year-old.

But these are superficial differences, no matter how heated the debate. Knitters bond together because we think about things that no one else cares about. We make stuff to show how much we love someone or how much we love the yarn or, like swimming the English Channel, just to see if we can.

For me, knitting wouldn't be as satisfying without this community of like-minded people, most of whom I know only in electronic form by reading their blogs or their comments in online communities like Ravelry or *Knitter's Review*. My life is richer because they have no qualms about copping to their needle habits. Their work frequently carries me through mine.

My husband and I joke that we are a "planning people."

We like goals and lists. Few things give me quite the same satisfaction as crossing something off a list or meeting a goal. If I meet a goal and *then* get to cross it off a list, the thrill is so great that I have to lie down until it passes. And I wonder why I'm not a big hit at parties.

To shorten this examination of my odd psyche, I am not a woman who enjoys process. I am a writer who does not enjoy writing. I can find innumerable ways to avoid it. But, to rip off Dorothy Parker, nothing else—nothing—gives me the same thrill as having written.

I'm the same way with knitting. The process is fine, mind you, and keeps my hands busy. But nothing else—nothing—gives me the rush that I get from finishing something.

The parallels between writing and knitting go even further. Like writing, knitting has a finite number of raw ingredients. There are twenty-six letters in the alphabet. Those letters can combine to give you David Foster Wallace or freshman composition papers. There are only two basic stitches: the knit and the purl. Those stitches can add up to a gorgeously complicated sweater or a pastel pink toilet paper cozy. The difference is in the mind that shapes them.

Which brings me to Alice Starmore, a knitwear designer whose garments are mind-numbingly gorgeous in both their beauty and complexity. To abuse my writing/knitting metaphor so much that it sulks off to the corner and begs for sweet mercy, Starmore is the Shakespeare of the knit and the purl.

To say that Starmore's designs are difficult oversimplifies them. The tricky language in a sonnet or a soliloquy hides a simplicity of emotion and theme that, once you can unlock it, blows you away with its genius. The same is true of most of Starmore's designs. Yes, the language is difficult to learn and speak, but the rewards are great, if you can manage to not set your entire project on fire because it drives you mad. Franklin Habit, author of *It Itches*, a book of knitting cartoons, and the Panopticon, a wildly popular knitting blog, says it best.

> I sat down with [Starmore's] *The Book of Fair Isle Knitting* and almost wet myself . . . So this is what makes people gaga over Fair Isle. The tension, the incredible chill-giving tension, of vibrant colors rippling in counterpoint to vigorous patterning, the two constantly pushing and pulling like opposing voices in a Baroque orchestral suite without ever tipping the balance.
>
> I kept on poring through [Starmore's] books, with their solid writing and their wildly creative variations on a theme, and I realized that for maybe the third time in my life I'd encountered an artist who was actually worthy of the hype. It's tough to design one good sweater, let alone a book full of them. It's damned near impossible to crank out a whole string of terrific books without going stale. And it's rare to find a scholar, a writer, and a designer all sharing the same body.

Beyond her jaw-droppingly impressive designs, Starmore herself is a source of controversy. She is the Edward Albee of the knitting world and appears to get her knickers in a bunch when knitters suggest modifications to her designs. Despite living on a relatively isolated Scottish island, she so vigorously protects her brand that many knitters avoid referring to her, lest she swoop in and sue when her name is invoked.

Given the names of some of her patterns—like St. Brigid, Anne of Cleves, Elizabeth I, and Henry VIII—you might expect Starmore to be a blousy, Miss Marple-ish, chintz-covered Briton of a certain age, but her legal fights show her to be tough.

If Starmore's feisty defense of her intellectual property weren't enough reason to turn away from her work, the patterns themselves might be. Starmore's Mary Tudor is a fiendishly difficult Fair Isle sweater whose mere mention can make a roomful of chatty women hush. Mary Tudor's intricate colorwork alternates bands of dusky purple and cobalt blue woven around heraldic symbols. The Mary Tudor is my Mount Everest. It is my Grail, my curse, and my compulsion. The quest to complete Mary Tudor—given that the pattern is out of print, the yarn has been discontinued, and the knitting is vast—can be the work of a lifetime. For a knitter who has only been knitting for a thimbleful of years, one who has been known to lose focus and knit two left mittens or count to twenty by skipping seventeen, Mary Tudor would be a foolish, humbling choice to attempt.

I want one.

I am not without common sense. I know how to make good choices. I floss. Taking on Mary Tudor right now would be silly. I have two children under the age of seven. I have a husband and a house and cats. I have two jobs at two separate colleges, plus whatever writing I can squeeze in around the fringes. My life is very full. Yet I feel like my very full life isn't progressing anywhere. I'm just running around in circles trying to keep all of life's balls in the air. I derive a certain amount of contentment from successfully doing that, but fighting a holding action against the slings and arrows of entropy doesn't bathe one in glory. Frankly, it leaves one only in need of a nap.

Crossing "kept wolves at bay" off a list gives me little joy. It's not what I would want as my epitaph. Other phrases that I hope don't appear in my obit include "kept a tidy house," "made a lovely roast chicken," "always returned student assignments in a timely fashion," and "ensured everyone had clean underpants." Those things are important—nothing harshes your day's mellow faster than dirty underpants—but I don't want them mentioned in a summary of my life.

Every New Year's Eve, rather than make resolutions that I have no intention of keeping, I pick one word on which to focus in the coming year. I write it on slips of paper, which invariably end up buried in piles on my desk, though they float to the surface periodically as I churn those piles during the year. Reminders like "Listen" or "Create" or "Patience" serve up a moment of silent contemplation as I reflect on how I'm doing. Our rituals help make us who we are.

One recent year I completely forgot to choose my word. I spent all of 2007 in a directionless haze but didn't notice its directionlessness until 2008 was hours away. I couldn't find any hints about what my word had been for 2007. Surely I had picked a word to focus on. It is what I do.

I cleaned my desk and found no hints. I did find the passbooks for the kids' savings accounts, however, so it wasn't a total waste of time.

I flipped though my calendar in order to find out just what I'd been doing for the last 365 days. I had spent a lot of time taking small people to various appointments. I had sent birthday cards. I had gone to work. The whole year had been a holding action. Nothing very bad or very good happened, which is nice in its own way. But I didn't accomplish anything that I could point to and say, "This is 2007." I didn't even have a word of the year written on my list.

Like I said, I am a planning person. Even though my life brings me contentment, I also need a challenge, one whose execution I can control. While my kids and my students and my spouse provide plenty of moments that test my patience and make me gird my loins, I am helpless before them. All I can control is my response. But with a sweater—say a fantastically complicated Fair Isle that will be stunning when it is done—I am in charge. The shots are mine to call as I climb the mountain with the wind blowing back my hair. My sherpas will be the knitters I know, whether in the virtual world or in real life.

Movement would be 2008's word. It was time for progress.

1
February
Knitting a Hat for No One

Cost of a cardigan sweater at Walmart: $13

I started my big complicated sweater by knitting a hat.

In order to explain fully why this makes complete sense, I'm going to make a quick left turn to give a quick and dirty overview of the mechanics of knitting. If you already know how to manipulate stick and string without putting out your own eye, this detour might be of limited value. It might not, though. One never knows.

In these halcyon Internet days, any method that produces a workable knit stitch is a keeper. Before knit blogs opened the conversation about the many ways there are to hold both sticks and string, there were two rigid schools for technique. A Continental knitter held her working yarn in her left hand and delicately picked it to create the next stitch. An English knitter held the working yarn in her right hand and brutally threw it to create the same.

Yes, the old squabbles between mainland Europe and the British Isles raise their ugly heads everywhere, even in the humble craft world. Adding to the international tensions is "combination knitting," which American designer Annie Modesitt codified during the last decade. Hard-core Continental and English knitters used to agree on only one thing: their way is the best. Now that the upstart combo knitting is gaining ground, however, the two have united against it, believing that the "enemy of my enemy is my friend." I offer this history merely as proof that no matter what you are doing, someone will be certain that you are doing it wrong.

I am an English knitter. I'd like to say that I learned to hold the working yarn in my right hand because that is inherently the right way to do it. In fact, I have no good reason for doing it that way, other than that was how the knitter in the pictures online held her yarn. I am living proof that it is possible to learn the basics of the craft online, skimming from site to site whenever something tricky comes along. No, the Internet isn't the best place to learn everything—I wouldn't turn there for an education in brain surgery or sex—but for a fairly simple craft, it's ideal.

Despite its appearance to nonknitters, knitting is fairly simple. You have two needles, one in each hand. When working with just one color, the working yarn is the strand that goes from your hand directly to the ball. You can drape that yarn over a finger (or fingers, if you wish) on your left or right hand.

Regardless of your knitting handedness, which frequently doesn't correspond with your writing handedness, a *knit* stitch is made when the right needle is inserted into a stitch on the left needle from front to back. The working yarn is wrapped over the right needle, then pulled from back to front of the left-hand stitch. For a *purl*, the working yarn is moved toward the knitter, the right needle goes through the front of the left-hand stitch, and the working yarn is wrapped around the right needle and pulled through. It sounds much more complicated than it is. Like, say, walking, which also sounds more involved than it is—lift heel of left foot, push off a wee bit with toes, shift balance, swing leg, etc.—knitting takes longer to explain than to show.

The short version is that, regardless of whether you drape your working yarn over your left hand or your right hand, the working yarn is either pulled from behind the first stitch on your left needle, which makes a knit stitch, or through the front of the first stitch, which makes a purl. That stitch is moved to the right needle and you now knit or purl the stitch that is in the first position on the left needle. That's it. As far as mysteries of the universe go, it's an easy one to unravel.

The above explanation doesn't hold true for the combination knitters. Since they are used to marginalization, I will continue mostly to ignore them here, not because their method is inferior but because it is not as easy to explain.

Even as an individual knitter follows one of the major schools of technique, she (or he) evolves her own interpretation of the style. Again, it's like walking. While we take similar steps—move right foot, move left foot, repeat—we each walk with our own gait. In knitting gait, I am an English knitter who picks rather than throws. Again, this is not because my method is superior. I just have very long index fingers.

At first, knitting feels like the most awkward thing you could be doing with your hands. The needles jump out of your hands. The yarn ties itself in knots. Your fingers act like an infant's when he tries to pick up a Cheerio. Knitting feels like the hardest easiest craft in the world. Practice, coupled with a willingness to look foolish, is what separates knitters from nonknitters.

To quote the great knitting sage Elizabeth Zimmerman, "Really, all you need to become a good knitter is wool, needles, hands and slightly below average intelligence. Of course, superior intelligence such as yours and mine is an advantage." Zimmerman, for what it's worth, was a Continental knitter, despite being British born.

Zimmerman is a legend in knitting circles, which you already know if you're a knitter. She moved to Wisconsin in the 1950s and fomented a quiet knitting renaissance with her PBS series, annual knitting camp, newsletter, and books. Zimmerman's fingers were in countless yarns. Able to knit on the back of her husband's motorcycle, Zimmerman, who died in 1999, approached the craft without fear and with a sense of adventure.

Which is also my approach to Mary Tudor—the sweater, not the princess. How hard can it be? I asked myself. I have superior intelligence. I have the entire Internet at my disposal. I can knit and purl. The worst that ever happens is that I start with a box of yarn and end with a box of yarn because I've unraveled all my work and given it up as bad juju.

My day-to-day life is full of actions that have larger potential consequences. I drive a minivan that could easily become a weapon if I flaked out for a millisecond. I teach young adults how to write, speak, and act responsibly in the larger world. I also teach my own small children how to become responsible young adults or, most days, how not to be the kid that all the other parents talk about in hushed, anxious tones. The consequences of screwing up a sweater are nil, which is a refreshing change. Of course, I had to up the stakes by giving myself a time limit—one year from a March 2008 start. Still, if I fail, no one dies.

All that only halfway explains why I started my sweater by knitting a hat. The other half of the story is a more romantic yarn that also involves fish guts, windswept islands, and chapped hands.

Knitting is a linear process. There are two primary ways to work a second (or third or fourth, depending on your stamina) color into a knitted item. Each row of stitches builds on the previous row of stitches, sort of like an old-school dot matrix printer. If you can't remember a time before cable TV and cell phones, go talk to an older person who can describe the dark days of monochromatic computer monitors and green-and-white printer paper. Then ask him how far he walked to school each morning.

Imagine that you are sitting on the ink cartridge of your printer. You are zipping along with your black ink when you come to several dozen dots that need to be hot pink. You hit the big brake pedal on the carriage. When you come to a complete stop, you pop out the black ink and kick it overboard.

You pop in the pink ink and continue on your way to the end of the row. Remember that printers aren't like typewriters; at the end of the row the carriage doesn't return to the beginning of the next line. Instead, it prints the next row in reverse order on top of the previous row. The carriage that you're sitting on moves up one line and, since you have not changed ink, prints out hot pink. When you get to the end of that color, you hit the brake and ditch the pink. Usually the black ink, which you left behind in the last row, is close to where you need it. You can just haul it onboard and go.

That technique is called *intarsia*. It's primarily used for blocks of color. Think of those Christmas sweaters with trees or stars or Scottie dogs all over them. The trees, etc., will be knitted intarsia-style. As with any technique, intarsia can be significantly more complicated than I've described. You can add more colors. You can add complicated patterns. Regardless, the key to intarsia is the dropping of one yarn and the picking up of another.

Mary Tudor is not an intarsia sweater. Instead, the colorwork is stranded. Rather than drop each yarn each time a new color is needed, you hold two colors simultaneously. If you are spatially oriented, you have already seen the problem with this method, especially if you go back to our dot matrix printer example. If each row is built upon the next, with one row always printing in reverse, it's silly to carry the black yarn through the pink bits when you won't need it until the middle of the next row, which is where it was waiting for you. And if you were knitting Fair Isle sweaters as flat sheets, that impulse to abandon the black yarn would get you a gold star.

Fair Isle, however, is knitted in the round, so the dot matrix printer analogy starts to fall apart. (Some would argue that it fell apart long ago. To you I say, "Shush.") Imagine taking your piece of printer paper and rolling it into a tube. The long sides should be flush. Now take an imaginary pencil—or an actual paper and pencil if, like me, manipulating shapes in your head makes you break out in a sweat—and draw a continuous line around the outside of your tube. When you come back to where you started, move the tip of your pencil so that it just brushes the top of what you've already drawn. Do this until you run out of paper.

That is how you knit an item in the round, which is how Fair Isle objects are worked. You are essentially knitting in a spiral, rather than rows. Leaving one yarn behind when you want to change colors makes little sense because it'll be in the wrong place when you need it again. Therefore, you have to carry all the colors you need with you as you go around and strand the unused yarn across the back of the stitches.

Traditional Fair Isle colorwork is also clever because it never uses more than two colors in any row. No matter how complex any pattern may look, any given row is a binary function. Either the stitch is color A or color B. The magic is how you stack these simple blocks.

The technique for speedy Fair Isle is simple as well. The knitter becomes both a British and a Continental knitter because she carries just one color in each hand. When she needs a black stitch, she plucks the black yarn. Ditto the hot pink. Simple is not the same as easy, mind you.

If you turn a piece of Fair Isle knitting inside out, you'll see all of those strands, which are also called *floats*. The floats make the finished garment extra warm because the knitter has essentially created two layers of insulation with each pass: the outside pattern and all the floats behind it. Since the yarn usually used for stranded knitting is thin and light, the finished product is down-jacket warm without all the down-jacket bulk.

Fair Isle sweaters have another unique feature: *steeks*. To understand steeks, imagine your cylinder of paper or wool again. As a cylinder, it will only fit a person without arms or one who doesn't mind having her arms pinned to her sides. In order to make armholes, Fair Isle knitters cut through the knitted tube, pick up stitches around the edges of the hole (now called a *steek*, because calling it a "big hole that I just cut in my knitting" lacks glamour), then knit merrily on to make sleeves.

It's a crazy idea, this steeking. Scissors and knitting go together like mashed potatoes and chocolate syrup. But the grippiness of Shetland wool makes possible steeking without unraveling, in all connotations of the word. Plus, the tradition of the steek allowed the Fair Isle knitters to churn out a sweater per week, which had an enormous impact on the economy in that corner of the cold ocean.

There is an actual Fair Isle. It is one of the islands in the Shetlands, which lurk above the Orkneys off Scotland's northeastern coast. Fair Isle shares its latitude with Homer, Alaska, and Bergen, Norway, which puts it almost on the Arctic Circle. Only fifteen of the hundred Shetland islands in the chain are inhabited. Despite their sparse population, the Shetlands are home to the most northernmost phone box in the UK; at press time, the number was 01957 711383 and international charges may apply. It's also home to Atlantic puffins and whooper swans, many of whom hang out in some of the more ebulliently named parts of the country. How could one resist a visit to Mavis Grind, Old Scatness, Mousa Broch, or Skaw?

In terms of hand knitting, however, there really is no distinction between Fair Isle and the rest of the islands. "It is possible but not very relevant to distinguish between the Fair Isle knitting of Fair Isle and the Fair Isle knitting of the rest of Shetland," writes Sheila McGregor in *Traditional Fair Isle Knitting*. "The purely 'Fair Isle' period lasted from about 1850 to 1910 or so; thereafter most other parts of Shetland began to produce very similar stranded knitting, using the old patterns of Fair Isle."

While currently part of the UK, the Shetlands could just as easily belong to Norway—and have at various points in history. Shetland Norn, the traditional tongue of the islands, now extinct, derived from Norwegian. Living that close to the Arctic Circle has taught the Shetlanders how to deal with the elements; those who didn't learn froze to death. (It's worth noting that there are few knitting traditions that spring from tropical climates. However, the Shetlands aren't known for their contributions to the world of fruity mixed drinks, sunscreen, or formal shorts. We all have our strengths.)

On those "Calgon, take me away" days, I dream of escaping to such an isolated Scottish island. Swathed in handknits,

I stare stonily into a brisk breeze, my long auburn locks streaming behind me. My flock of sheep grazes picturesquely in the background. Waves and the rough tearing of the grass that the sheep crop are the only sounds.

As with so many dreams, the reality of island life in the Shetlands is less romantic. While the Shetlands see their share of blustery days, they aren't as bitter or blizzardy as they could be because of the warming effects of the Gulf Stream. The islands do corner the market in all forms of cold damp. The islands receive, on average, 60 days of snowfall and 285 days of other precipitation per year. On those 20 days when something isn't falling out of the sky, I might be tempted to hide inside all day, because the sight of clear skies would be so unusual.

They lack sun, but the islands have a surfeit of natural wonders. Even so, the Reverend James Kay, the minister of an island parish in the 1600s, noted that "there are no Forrests, Woods, nor Parks here . . . no Lochs, no Rivers, no Trees, no Broom, no Whins." For those not conversant with seventeenth-century Scotts, broom and whins are brambly plants. If that weren't enough to keep you from a visit, the islands also have boat-eating tides and, until recently, a distinct lack of hospitals. In the 1880s, a visitor to the islands warned his countrymen to pack "a pocket enema, as alteration in diet, and what not, are apt to bring on violent constipation."

The above quotes are from Valerie M. Thom's *Fair Isle: An Island Saga*, which is great reading and gives real dirt on the practical side of living on a small, subarctic island. Like this bit: "Infrequent contact with the outside world meant that the islanders had little resistance to infection, so that any common school-age complaint, once introduced, was likely to become an epidemic, affecting all age groups." Way to be a buzzkill, Thom. I doubt that Fair Isle's tourist brochures frequently cite her.

Currently, the Shetland Islands' biggest moneymaker is the oil industry, and many folks will put up with all manner of hardships in order to get their hands on sweet crude. The North Sea covers some rich deposits of the black gold, and Lerwick, capital of the Shetland Islands, is a convenient port. But the global oil market is a relatively recent economic incentive and, before oil, the biggest sources of income for the islanders were fish and handknits.

The islands have a lot of sheep, most of which are a breed now known as the Shetland. Not coincidentally, the Shetland Islands are also home to the Shetland sheepdog, which looks like a miniature collie. Like a stranded Fair Isle sweater, Shetland sheepdogs have two layers of warmth: a rough outer coat and a fluffy inner layer. On these compact, rocky islands, nature and human hands have selected animals for their hardiness and stature. In many ways, the adjective *Shetland* is code for "low to the ground and hard to knock over." The appellation also nicely describes the Shetland pony and the Shetland goose.

Shetland sheep are known for their hardiness and for their wool, which is relatively soft and naturally grows in a variety of colors, as long as the variety of colors you're looking for is browns, blacks, or grays. Writes Thom, "Characteristic too is the Shetland's goat-like agility, enabling it to graze apparently inaccessible grassy cliff-ledges and descend precipitous paths to feed on seaweed—habits which sometimes result in a sheep becoming stuck and having to be rescued. It was when a would-be rescuer slipped and had to be rescued himself that the islanders earned the Carnegie Hero Award displayed in the Community Hall."

The rescue, by the way, took place in 1956 on, of course, a wet night. The cliff in question had long been considered unscalable. The would-be rescuer lay on a rock shelf with a broken thigh while three of his countrymen descended two hundred feet, strapped him to a stretcher, then hauled him back up. After that, the rescued shepherd had to be loaded onto the island's main ferry to be shipped to the mainland.

Which tells you two things: the Fair Islanders are incredibly stout people and they really love their sheep.

Where there are sheep, there are knitters. Thom points out that the earliest record of the craft in the islands dates from the mid-1700s, when a ship's captain noted in his log that the women were "continually employed in knitting stockings or gloves and spinning woolen yarn." By 1774 the women were trading "knit caps, mittens, stockings and the softest coarse cloth I ever saw made of wool."

Knitting is what women did for fun as well as profit, and they even knit during the biggest social events on the island. For events called *lifts*, groups of islanders would gather to cut peat, which isn't code for more nefarious activities but rather means standing in the middle of a bog, lifting and cutting the moss that grows on its surface to dry and use for fuel. After the day's labor, there would be dinner and folktales.

My favorite of these stories involves a monster named Grotti Finnie, who may or may not have been in a battle with a pig for a stuffed fish stomach (think haggis but with extra offal). I was too busy rolling the name Grotti Finnie around in my head to pay attention to all the details. Even after their strenuous workout in the bogs, "the women's hands would not be allowed to lie idle; the oil lamps gave plenty of light for spinning and knitting. The lift was, however, an occasion when the men did not work at making straw baskets and chairbacks, but simply reminisced and played cards." Knowing Thom as I've come to, I can almost hear her derisive snort while she typed that last bit.

The men's talk is lost in time, but the women's has been passed down through the generations and includes natural cures for everyday indignities, rhymes for making a cow's milk come more easily, and Fair Isle patterns. If you sub in "potty training" or "public schools" for "cow's milk," you've just described a fair amount of the conversation that floats around knitting circles.

In addition to the social aspects of knitting, this women's work accomplished during their "idle hours" turned into a moneymaker. "In common with most other parts of Scotland where there was a supply of suitable wool, hand knitting rapidly developed into a major cottage industry in the sixteenth and later centuries," writes McGregor, who doesn't have quite the same sardonic zest as Thom. "The main articles produced for trade were coarse stockings in enormous numbers, together with such other small items and nightcaps, waistcoats (i.e. knitted underwear) and gloves." One hopes that the aforementioned softest coarse cloth was reserved for underpant fabrication.

While the handknit industry tanked on mainland Scotland thanks to the nineteenth-century proliferation of knitting machines, it remained a going concern in the Shetlands for most of the twentieth century. Hand knitting's survival there has less to do with the island's isolation than with the ingenuity of the knitters in question. Once these fiberworkers started using vegetable-based dyes to expand their color palettes, Fair Isle knitting became distinct.

Before the oil boom, knitted goods were one of the few exports from the islands. The poor, rocky soil did not yield many crops, and overfishing had depleted the waters around the islands. But those sturdy sheep and those industrious hands remained constant. "The remarkable achievements of the hand knitters of nineteenth-century Fair Isle, who produced brilliant and exciting knitting in surroundings of extreme poverty and hardship, deserve more credit than is generally given," writes McGregor.

By the end of the nineteenth century, the work of those hands grew increasingly in demand. During the 1886 International Exhibition in Edinburgh, the Fair Islanders' distinctive patterns were singled out for their complexity and beauty. What pushed the popularity of these garments over the top—like Michelle Obama wearing a pair of J. Crew gloves—was the Prince of Wales wearing a Fair Isle sweater while golfing at St. Andrews in 1921. Historians aren't certain of the genesis of these patterns: one story suggesting they had been learned from shipwrecked Spaniards in 1588 appears to be apocryphal. But their unique designs kept the islanders employed until the 1980s, when these sweaters became too dear to produce when compared with cheaper, machine-knitted versions. To add insult to injury, the distinctive Fair Isle patterns proved easy to knock off and hard to copyright. The tradition appeared to be at death's door, sustained by the smallest of rescue breaths from the knitters on the islands who'd always made their sweaters that way.

What snatched Fair Isle patterns from obscurity was a growing base of hand knitters, who finally had enough experience under their needles to seek out new challenges and to reconnect with old traditions. "Hand knitting, once a major British industry, has regained much of its former respectability since the days, not long ago, when it was described as a suitable occupation only for the aged and feeble-minded," McGregor wrote in 1981. Into that void stepped Alice Starmore.

The Isle of Lewis, Starmore's home, is not in the Shetlands, by the way. It's in the Hebrides, the chain that is also off the coast of Scotland but to the northwest rather than the extreme northeast. Lewis itself is just north of (and, technically, attached to) the Isle of Harris, the source for Harris tweed. The largest city in the area is Stornoway. But more about Alice in a bit. Right now, I'm telling you about the hat.

My first step to knitting Mary Tudor is to teach myself how to knit in the most effective Fair Isle style, which is in the round (remember that cylindrical piece of paper) and with one color of yarn in each hand (remember the two printer inks carried simultaneously).

I'm a big fan of circular knitting and use it in every application I can justify. I'm so comfortable with knitting tubes that I worked on a sock, which is essentially a big tube with a heel, during my second child's labor. When I couldn't remember how to knit anymore, I knew the boy was serious about his dramatic entrance. I'm told that my knit-and-purl habit was the talk of the nurses' station that night.

I've never carried one color of yarn in each hand. While stranded technique is simple in theory, teaching my fingers to do it is less so. My right hand cooperates; my left flails about like a trout on a hook. If I'd learned to play the piano as a kid, I might be better at this. As it is, forcing my left hand to work in concert with my right is making my eyes cross.

I come from the tough-love school of physiological functions. I'd just as soon bull through a day as grab a nap. Warm-ups are for sissies; if you're going to run, just run already. I don't coddle colds or ice sprains. This may be why I am frequently sick and limping.

I'm not proud of this attitude, but part of being an adult is accepting truth. And the truth is that I am the last person you want to go to for sympathy when you have the flu.

Rather than force my left hand to suck it up and get with the program by jumping right into the Mary Tudor, I decide to go back to basics. I'd like to say that this decision is owing to a great leap in maturity, but honestly, I have neither pattern nor yarn for the Mary Tudor yet. While a lack of direction and materials usually doesn't stop me, I realize that some remedial knitting practice is in order.

I'll knit a hat, I think, and only work Continental style.

The working yarn will never leave my nonpreferred hand. If I'm feeling kicky, I'll toss in some rows of two-handed work. A plain old knitted hat usually takes an evening or two, depending on how many times I get interrupted. A left-handed plain old knitted hat can't take more than a week.

I'm cheered by this thought from Stephanie Pearl-McPhee, who has become a knitting rock star with her books and her blog, yarnharlot.ca. McPhee's latest title, *Free-Ranger Knitter*, was a *New York Times* best seller, which speaks volumes about both her popularity and that of the craft.

(Pearl-McPhee also made the *Times* in 2007, where her coining of the word *Kinnearing* earned her an entry in a neologism roundup. *To Kinnear*, writes Grant Barrett, is "to take a candid photograph surreptitiously, especially by holding the camera low and out of the line of sight. Coined in August by Stephanie Pearl-McPhee of the Yarn Harlot blog when she attempted to take a photograph during an encounter with the actor Greg Kinnear at an airport." Kinnear himself would later go on to call Pearl-McPhee the "Michael Jordan of knitting" on *Late Night with Conan O'Brien.*)

"Maybe it's because knitting has such a rich and varied history," Pearl-McPhee writes in *Things I Learned from Knitting (Whether I Wanted To or Not)*. "Maybe it's because so many knitters have finished projects that prove they're successful (this point can be demoralizing if you're not currently enjoying knitting success). Or maybe it's because knitting was considered child labor until the turn of the century (and remains so in some parts of the world). Most knitters will eventually come to believe that there is very little they can't accomplish in knitting. They might not be able to do it now, they might not be able to do it for some time, but generally speaking, if a human possesses the intelligence and hand-eye coordination to read and write at a minimum level, then he is capable of being a darned solid knitter."

A quick rummage through my yarn closet—yes, I have an entire closet devoted to yarn—unearths two balls of worsted-weight wool left over from some long-forgotten project. I grab the navy ball. The first six rows look like they were knitted by a blue jay that was simultaneously fighting off a house cat, the image of which I am familiar with because of Barney, my black and white cat who has no respect for the sanctity of life. One of knitting's biggest advantages is that you can always go back to your starting point by pulling out your needles and unwinding your work. This can also be one of knitting's biggest disadvantages if you live with other people or animals. I rip it out.

Days pass because my response to wanting to learn a new skill is to ignore it until the urge goes away.

I grab the gray ball because the navy ball clearly has some bad chi. My work is better—it looks only like it was mangled by a house cat—but every other stitch is mounted on the needle backward and I have no idea why. I pull it out again.

Days pass, because I am avoiding casting on yet again. This shouldn't be so difficult. I know how to knit. I have a long history of successfully knitting things. Still, just the idea of forcing my left hand to cooperate makes me want to sob a little bit.

I grab the navy ball and realize one of the small people in

the house has stolen my needles. Hours pass while I sweat the information out of my daughter, who was using them to poke deep but narrow holes in the backyard. I wash them off.

I grab the navy ball again, which is starting to mat and fray from all the action. I complete two decent-looking inches in nearly three hours. An average hat is ten to twelve inches long. My muscles in my left forearm ache, as does my head, because nothing about my favorite hobby feels natural when I switch hands. This may take a little longer than I thought.

2

March

Acquisitions, or You Spent *How Much on a Book?*

Cost of a copy of Alice Starmore's *Tudor Roses*: $134.03

A blue and white U.S. Postal Service Priority Mail box is sitting in my office, where it has been for two days, mocking me. I'm afraid to open it and I keep moving it from my favorite green chair to my desk, then back to the chair or onto the floor. Like a kid on Christmas morning, I'll give it a shake now and again. But I can't bring myself to open it. Barney has shown more interest in releasing its contents than I have. Every now and again he'll take a break from his busy napping schedule to chew on the tape around the edges. Freak.

What stops me each time I go to open it is the knowledge that I'm one step closer to my dream sweater. Once I break the seal, I'll have to start. I'll have to let this sweater become my constant companion for the next year. And because I lack the sense that the good Lord gave a cabbage, I've committed myself to writing about the experience. I'll have 365 days to complete both book and sweater.

I've already learned one big lesson: I have exactly the wrong personality to enjoy eBay auctions. My nerves can't take the last-minute flurry of bidding. Fifteen minutes before the auction for a *Tudor Roses* book (which has the Mary Tudor pattern in it) ended, I thought I'd get my book for ninety bucks. Then, oh then, I realized I was in for $130. It all happened so fast, what with the clicking and the hyperventilating and the panic.

Next thing, I was left shaking and clammy and looking for booze, which reminded me of college.

With all that excitement, you'd think I'd rip into the package once I got it home from the post office. Yet the box is still here, unopened. Acting very *2001* monolith-like but more nonchalant. It makes me wonder if I should throw a monkey into it. Or was that a bone? I never did get the point of that movie.

I should have torn into the box when I first picked it up. Then it wouldn't have built up this mighty symbolic status in my mind.

The clerk didn't even ask for ID. "I know who you are," she said, and laughed. I said, "It's scary that I'm in here enough to be known," and laughed back. But it is scary. Even though I live in a small town, I didn't think I could become a fixture at the PO, like some Eudora Welty character. Seriously. I'm not there that much, am I?

I didn't rip into the box there because the time just hadn't felt ripe enough. I needed supplies first.

Before I could set off on this journey, I had to get a new journal, because nothing thrills me more than a trip to my office supply store. I can spend hours among all those rows of Post-its and paper clips. I can easily kill a morning just looking at pens—and do, while the box waits in the passenger seat. Will it be gel ink this time? Roller ball? Fuschia ink or plain old blue? This is not a decision one should rush. Unlike, say, the decision to knit a big-ass sweater and write a book about the process. *That* you should rush headlong into. But a pen is important.

I have my pen, a blue, gel ink Tul. It's nice, not my pen soul mate but good enough. I have a place to keep all the reams of notes I'm sure to make. I'm now out of excuses.

I open the box.

I'm giddy and want to throw up. This just can't be normal.

According to the packing slip, my copy of *Tudor Roses* was previously owned by Rita Petteys, a Michigan knitter. "I hope you love this book," she wrote on the invoice. "The patterns are amazing. I just never found the time to knit them. Take care and happy knitting!"

Petteys isn't in the used book business, as it turns out. She is, however, in the yarn business. Yarn Hollow, her home-based operation, specializes in hand-dyed yarns, roving (unspun wool), fabric, patterns, and finished goods. Yarn Hollow yarns are carried in half a dozen shops in Michigan and Indiana and online.

Because I can't resist talking to knitters (and because there was a phone number on the invoice), I called Petteys to find out where my pricey book had come from. I was hoping for a story involving Russian spies and the black market. But the truth was much simpler.

"I bought it when it first came out," Petteys says. "The company I worked at gave a five-year anniversary gift, so I had this extra money. I went and bought *Tudor Roses* and a packet of yarn to make one of the sweaters, the Catherine of Aragon cardigan, I think. I bought it at Threadbender in Wyoming, Michigan.

"I sold the yarn pack in 2004 because I came to the realization that I love Fair Isle knitting and I love Alice Starmore designs but at that time we were expecting our second child and I needed some baby gear. I sold the yarn on eBay, then ended up buying a bedside Co-Sleeper. The yarn was kind of rare at that point, so I got a lot of money for it. I hung on to the book because I knew that Jamieson had similar yarns. I thought, 'Oh, well, maybe someday I'll be able to do an Alice Starmore design.' I really do think they're beautiful. But then the realities of life made me think, 'You know, I've had this book for ten years and I haven't done anything with it yet, so it's time to let it go.'"

Petteys was surprised by how much the book sold for. And, naturally, excited by how much it sold for. She didn't need another bedside sleeper, though. "This time around, in between having my second child and selling the book, I had started my own business. It paid for supplies," she says.

Like me, Petteys learned to knit as a child but didn't get serious about it until she was older.

"I did a little bit in high school, then like one project in college, a scarf or something," she says. "I started knitting again in 1991, when my after-college roommate wore a sweater and my boyfriend admired it. I said, 'Oh, I can knit you that sweater.' I took the pattern to knitting class and said, 'I want to knit this.' It was at a time when young people weren't knitting. So I've been earnestly knitting since about 'ninety-one."

At the time, Petteys didn't know about the boyfriend sweater curse, one of those bits of knitterly lore that gets handed down through the generations. It is believed that knitters who start a sweater for a boyfriend will break up with him before it's done. The exact workings of the curse are unclear, but there are two schools of thought: 1) sweaters take a long time to knit and most relationships peter out before the sweater is done, and 2) deciding to knit a sweater for a significant other costs less than having a baby when it feels like the relationship is already in trouble.

The boyfriend sweater can also be used offensively. If you are too chicken to directly break up with someone, just start a sweater and events will take care of themselves. Little is known, sadly, about the impact of the boyfriend sweater curse on same-sex relationships.

And, yes, knitters do put this kind of thought into such topics. Given the repetitiveness of the craft, your mind has freedom to wander.

Curse be damned, Petteys and her then-boyfriend are now married with two kids. But her return to knitting set her up for a few decades (and more, one hopes) of satisfaction.

"I knit at the time because I didn't really have anything to do and I needed a hobby. The thing was, when I had the time, I had no money. Now I knit gifts for people. I knit to create designs for my company and I knit to try new things. It's a good way to relax at the end of the day. It's something to look forward to," Petteys says.

Petteys's experience with Fair Isle, however, has been less enjoyable. Petteys made a sweater created by Philosopher's Wool, a Canadian company that designs and assembles kits for their own style of Fair Isle garments. It didn't turn out as she'd hoped. "I would call that one probably the hardest project because of the right-hand-left-hand thing," she says. I try to not panic because this is the exact same problem I'm having with my left-hand-only hat.

I assure myself that I'll be okay because her project had additional portents. "I didn't realize my gauge was too small, so I used up too much yarn. So I made a sweater that's unwearable to me. My sister, who is smaller, can wear it but it's not really her. I would call that hard in terms of I didn't like the end product and the time it took."

This is exactly the sort of tidbit that makes me wonder how my own first attempt at a big Fair Isle project will go horribly wrong. My hope is that I won't lose an eye.

The question that you're asking yourself is, "Why did you need eBay to find a copy of *Tudor Roses*? Why not just buy a copy of the book from your local yarn shop?" Actually, your question may really be, "You paid *how* much for a book of knitting patterns?"

The answer to the first two questions is where my simple project of knitting a very complicated sweater becomes almost Dickensian in its scope. As for the answer to the last one, my only response is, *"I know."*

Alice Starmore, in addition to being a real, live, breathing person, is also a trademarked brand. And person Alice Starmore is ferocious about protecting brand Alice Starmore, so much so that it becomes increasingly difficult to separate one from the other. Knitters who admire Starmore's work have grown increasingly wary of mentioning her name, choosing instead to call her Litigious Scottish Designer (or LSD) or She Who Must Not Be Named (SWMNBN). Many fear that, like Lord Voldemort, SWMNBN's lawyers will swoop from the heavens to curse the innocent upon the mere mention of Starmore's name.

"There's still an ongoing joke online. Everyone's like, 'Don't mention her name!'" says Jenna Wilson, a Canadian copyright lawyer who has been documenting the legal travails of the knitting world. And yes, this humble craft, long thought to be the purview of gentle old ladies, can be fierce when it comes to interknitter squabbles and turf wars. A section of Wilson's website, girlfromauntie.com, is devoted to what she calls "The Alice Chronicles."

The easiest place to start untangling the issues that bind Starmore the person and Starmore the brand is in 1994. By this point in her career, Starmore's designs were well known and beloved, so much so that she had been a frequent visitor to U.S. yarn shops, conventions, and trade organizations since the late 1980s. (She later wrote about her heady first days in the spotlight in *Road Movies Volume 1*, which was released in 2008 by Windfall Press, her own imprint.)

While I was just starting my useless postcollege twenties in the mid-1990s, Starmore launched her own eponymous yarn line and offered five compositions of yarn: Scottish Heather, Scottish Fleet, Dunedin, Bainin, and Scottish Campion. A full breakdown of each yarn's pros and cons is left as an exercise for the truly devoted; however, here's a Cliff Notes version: all these yarns are 100 percent wool. What makes each unique is its intended purpose, which can be sussed out from the yarn's weight. Scottish Heather is a worsted-weight yarn for relatively quick-knitted single-color sweaters. Scottish Fleet is a lighter weight, which means smaller needles, best used in gansey-style sweaters. Dunedin is a fingering-weight yarn for gloves, socks, or scarves. Bainin is perfect for cabled sweaters. And Scottish Campion is ideal for stranded Fair Isle cardigans like Mary Tudor.

Designing knitwear patterns—no matter what the end garment—is a careful dance between designer, manufacturer, and distributor, who is frequently also a publisher. Most designers, like Starmore at the beginning of her career, don't work with their own yarns and are beholden to other companies to provide the media for their vision. Not only does the yarn maker provide the raw materials for the designer; the company has to keep that specific blend of yarn in stock for anyone else who might want to make the pattern after seeing it in a magazine or a book or, increasingly, online.

The business end of the craft is a knotted-up skein. Envision a lonely designer sketching a pattern on the back of her electric bill. What will she need? She will need yarn, of course, but will also have to keep in mind that other knitters will need access to this yarn too. She'll also need a way to get the pattern to the knitters who like her work. In the pre-Internet days, distribution was usually through publication in magazines, books, or pamphlets. These end products used to be found only in yarn shops, whose owners dealt largely with bigger distributors. It's not an altruistic system, of course. The shop owners don't want patterns that no one wants to knit. The manufacturers won't sell much yarn unless big-name designers write patterns that are published in leading magazines. While there is communication between each of these entities—publishers will suggest certain yarns to designers in order to satisfy a manufacturer that will pull its advertising if it doesn't have its product featured, say—each leg of this stool has its own interests and fiercely protects them. If a yarn producer kills a line that a designer uses heavily, then that designer's fans (and potential fans) are out of luck. Yarn shops miss out on potential sales and will start stocking patterns from a designer whose materials can be easily found by customers.

Starmore's Dunedin, etc., yarns were born out of this need, at least in part. Her earliest designs call for yarns that their manufacturer, a British company named Rowan, couldn't keep fully stocked and ultimately discontinued. Those knitters who stashed these yarns can ask (and receive) hundreds of dollars for these skeins.

Before the deaths of those Rowan yarns, however, Starmore had already begun to concentrate on using only her own yarns in her patterns. First, contracting a mill to produce her own yarns would give Starmore more control over the colors and spin. Second, Starmore would have more control over the availability of her yarns, which would funnel more cash into her pocket. With the release of her brand of yarn, Starmore had roped two legs of the stool together. But she didn't quite have a handle on the publishing of her work yet, which would soon become a problem.

Two books, *In the Hebrides* (1995) and *Tudor Roses* (1998), rely heavily on these branded yarns, and the Fair Isle garments—Starmore is also known for her ingenious cabled designs—in these books are stunning. The colors shift and flow voluptuously with an interplay between incongruent tones—like a warm acid green and a lush cool purple in Mary Tudor—that make you realize that you really don't understand color theory at all. If you focus on any one square inch of a pattern, it looks like a garish mess. Focus on the whole picture and it takes your breath away.

This triumph of design would have been nearly impossible without Starmore's taking charge of the raw materials of her craft. No sensible knitter can begrudge Starmore her artistic need for control. No, but sensible knitters can hold a grudge about what came next.

Scottish Campion was initially produced by Jamieson and Smith, a woolen mill based in Lerwick in the Shetland Islands. For reasons that remain out of the public record, Starmore moved production of Campion to another mill, confusingly also named Jamieson (but without a Smith) that is also in the Shetlands, in Sandness, rather than Lerwick.

Confused yet? It gets worse. You might want to draw yourself a map. In Europe, these yarns were distributed by Jamieson. In the United States, they were distributed by the Broad Bay Company, which also handled the books *In the Hebrides* and *Tudor Roses*. But ours is not to reason why. Ours is but to report that through some disagreements between the distributors and Starmore about control over her colors, craft, and designs, Starmore chose to pack up her toys and go home, metaphorically speaking.

As she memorably wrote, "I am not prepared to play the meek little woman. . . . Circumstances have led in this direction, especially after so many years of hard work in writing, designing, teaching and generally building up Alice Starmore yarns. However, these circumstances dictate that there is only one course to take, and that is the course of action that I invariably follow whenever I discover a mistake in my knitting—take it out and start again, even if the piece is only a couple of rows from completion. It is the only way to remain true to the art. So I will apply my own knitting philosophy and do now what hindsight shows I should have done back in October 1998—start again," Starmore wrote.

With that parting shot, Starmore's business relationships with her yarn distributors and book publishers was dissolved as of August 2000. Her choice is understandable, almost admirable, as if she'd left a marriage in which she believed that she was being abused. If that's where the saga ended, knitters would be disappointed, I suspect, but get over it and follow Starmore wherever she decided to go next. Now would be a great time to cue up some ominous music on your iPod.

Left in limbo after the split was the finished manuscript for *25 Years*, a new book of patterns and essays that celebrated Starmore's twenty-fifth year in the business. Also in limbo were all the yarn shop owners who no longer had anyone to order from and all the knitters smitten by the patterns in *In the Hebrides* and *Tudor Roses*. Once the publisher ran out of its stock, those titles began to command high dollars in the resale market.

Soon Starmore turned her ire toward the knitters who still wanted to knit the designs in the books that their writer had declared dead and that their distributor could no longer support. Yet even as Starmore did her best to distance herself from her books, more and more knitters were falling in love with her designs.*

Knitters are can-do people. As Elizabeth Zimmerman wrote in *Knitting Without Tears*, knitting's "main tenets are enjoyment and satisfaction accompanied by thrift, inventiveness, an appearance of industry, and above all, resourcefulness."

In short, knitters are not the sort to balk at a challenge, especially when that challenge involves mere yarn and needles. If global warming and the Israeli/Palestinian conflict could be solved with knitting, we'd already have happy polar

---

* Again, I have to note that Jenna Wilson, girl from auntie and lawyer, has written on her blog the definitive examination of these interactions between Starmore and the world. My intention is limited to hitting the highlights, mostly because I am not a lawyer, nor do I play one on TV.

bears and peace in the Middle East. Tell us that a yarn has been discontinued and we'll figure out another way to make a project work, even if we have to shear our own sheep and dye our own yarns. And we'll tell all our friends how to do it too, which seems to be the burr under Starmore's saddle.

Judging from the outside, it starts to look like Starmore took a scorched earth policy toward those who still wanted to make items from her past works. Knitters wouldn't play along with the idea of not knitting the patterns in *In the Hebrides* and *Tudor Roses.* While the Back Bay bathwater may have soured, Starmore's wonderful babies didn't need to be chucked out as well, from a knitterly perspective.

The Internet, that fabulous series of tubes, has made sharing our knitting adventure with the like-minded vastly easier. In April 2001 a knitter started a Yahoo! group called alicestarmore. Discussions about yarn substitutions for her increasingly hard-to-find yarns, including Starmore's Campion, thrived on the group. As new members joined, those who asked were brought up to speed on the legal sitch up to that point.

In February of 2002, for reasons unknown, the owner of the Yahoo! group decided that all discussions about Starmore's past as well as about ways to substitute yarns with other, non-Starmore brands were verboten. Members and posts were moderated. Those who expressed an opinion about Starmore's decisions regarding her former distributors were also bounced by the moderators.*

---

* This group is now called starmoreknitters and is still moderated.

The idea of not being able to talk about a knitting project rankled the knitters who still wanted to make these gorgeous garments. Knitters being knitters, another group was started to talk about these topics. Sheila Hansford spearheaded the Alice Starmore Open Forum, where discussion was freewheeling. This group and its archives have been deleted from Yahoo!'s servers, and the reasons for its erasure from the record start to explain how Starmore bludgeoned her reputation with her own metaphorical needles.

In 2001, before the days of everyone having a blog, a Starmore devotee who called herself Ciscospice published an online diary of her experience with knitting Starmore's pattern called Luskentyre. Included was a photo of Ciscospice's work in progress and a scan of her working copy of the chart. She used the items to illustrate some tips for making Fair Isle easier. The pages included attribution for the design.

Ciscospice emailed Starmore's newly opened online retail shop, Virtual Yarns, which went live in 2001, to get an okay for using these images. The answer was no. Shortly thereafter, noncommercial pages—those created by knitters—that offered suggestions of substitutions for the unavailable yarn were targeted with "you'd better stop" letters as well.

In February 2002 Hansford also received a cease-and-desist email, contending that the name Alice Starmore, the initials AS, and the name Alice were protected under Starmore's trademark. This letter was later submitted to the Electronic Frontier Foundation (EFF), an advocacy group for education about the legitimate scope of U.S. intellectual property laws. Hansford's return email requested specific examples of her misuse of the Starmore marks. No reply came.

Interestingly, shortly after this, Hansford placed an order at Virtual Yarns. The next day it was canceled due to "current circumstances."

"The inference was obvious to those of us who heard about the cancellation," writes Jenna Wilson. "Sheila did attempt to coax some further explanation of the 'current circumstances' by emailing Starmore directly, but no reply to this second message was received, either."

On February 26, the chat group was expunged from Yahoo!'s servers by Yahoo!, yet Wilson and other members of the group still don't know exactly how the Alice Starmore Open Forum violated Yahoo!'s terms of service. Hansford immediately started another Yahoo! group, this one named ASOF, and resubscribed all the former group's members. She also published the correspondence between Starmore's representative and herself.

Response was mixed. Some group members decided to boycott Virtual Yarns, some cautioned that it was best to separate designer from designs, and some wondered why a designer would alienate those who love her work. A few felt Hansford was in the wrong for talking about an issue that Starmore didn't want to talk about. Folks mused about what rights a designer retains over a pattern once it has been purchased. Knitters, in short, kibitzed about the whole kerfuffle.

Hansford and other ASOF members were concerned that

the group would again be deleted at the request of a third party (which it was), so Hansford shifted all their content to a new site called Knitting Beyond the Hebrides, which is still in existence and has had no legal action taken against it. There, knitters talk about Starmore's designs and those of other knitters exploring a similar theme. Then came eBay.

In May 2002 an auction for a knitted garment—which had been made with the knitter's own yarn and labor using a Starmore pattern—was canceled by eBay because it had received a complaint alleging that it violated Starmore's intellectual property. Other auctions—especially those that mentioned both the names Jamieson and Starmore yarn—vanished. The list of disappeared auctions included those for yarn packs (assembled by yarn shops and containing just yarn and not a pattern) and kits with patterns (usually a yarn pack and a copy of the book with the pattern in it).

The triggers for complaints were nebulous. Some auctions that included Starmore yarns breezed through. Others didn't. Members of KBTH puzzled through what constituted an infringement. Since all it took at the time to get the auction pulled was one complaint from a third party—the force of such a complaint was never tested in court—the standing of these auctions with regard to Starmore's trademark is still far from clear.

Hansford, whose doggedness I admire, hired an attorney, Robert Ward of Seed IP Law Group in Seattle, who provided guidance for the group on what they could and could not sell on eBay. Hansford and like-minded individuals started to auction Starmore-related items for a legal action fund (LAF), which was used to defray some of the costs. Most of the items were tokens, like a shell from the Isle of Lewis, which is where Starmore makes her home. The group raised more than two thousand dollars.

Hansford's auctions, however, still kept getting canceled by eBay. Starmore's representative, Alexander Muir, did not make clear how these auctions—the wording of which Hansford had had cleared by her lawyer—in his view broke the law. At the time, eBay had no provision for challenging third parties who did not prove how the item in question infringed on their trademark.

Things seemed to be at a stalemate. Hansford kept putting up auctions, which eBay would remove because a third party complained that they violated her intellectual property rights. EBay and the third party would never state exactly what constituted the infringement. Then Lisa Latham, a journalist from the *Seattle Times*, wrote a story about the whole brouhaha in 2003.

From Latham's story:

> [Starmore's U.S. attorney Susan Upton] Douglass contends Starmore has no objection to "fair and nondeceptive uses of her name to promote genuine merchandise." But harming her reputation "by confusing or misleading others is not permissible," she says.
>
> "Mrs. Hansford needs to get a life. Her endless sniping and jealous rage are getting tiresome," Douglass says.
>
> Hansford says the group is trying to treat a serious situation with humor. "It would be very easy to become bitter

and angry about this, so we're trying to assert our rights with a smile on our faces," she says.

The first Douglass quote comes from a letter to Hansford on December 4, 2002, in which the attorney outlines Starmore's position. The major point of argument is that eBay sellers had alleged that certain yarns of Jamieson's Shetland Spindrift collection were the same in both color and construction as the discontinued Campion yarn. From Jenna Wilson's gloss: "The letter goes on to suggest that those who wished to create the original Starmore design with substitute yarns would be disappointed and deceived, in violation of U.S. trademark law."

Despite repeated volleys of lawyer letters, the argument was, for all intents and purposes, dead by January 2003. Auctions stopped being pulled. Hansford left KBTH. Unused LAF funds were returned.

Why this argument abruptly died is unclear. Hansford and company were prepared to keep pressing the issue, but Starmore stopped pushing back. No one is clear what the law will actually permit because these alleged infringements never went to court. Perhaps Starmore decided that these were minor problems and she had larger projects to spend energy on; perhaps she realized that she was causing her own brand harm by attacking those who love it. Starmore also got caught up in a dispute about a mill around the same time. In any case, Starmore's zealous protection of her trademark had left a bad taste.

"Part of the problem all the way through has been that she

might be right," Wilson tells me in 2009. "Some of the things that she might have said or her agent might have said might be right or might be wrong. The general problem overall is that there's a chilling effect. Some people really are afraid to talk about Alice Starmore online. They are afraid of what's going to happen. Nobody really knows what the law is or which country's law applies to all of these online transactions."

"Once I did get an email from Alice Starmore," Wilson says. "I can't remember if it was before or during or after I first published the Alice Chronicles. She actually sent me a nice email thanking me for having the copyright FAQ for knitters on my website. There was some comment in her email about how some knitters don't understand copyright or that they thought that knitting patterns were free for the taking or something like that."

So why, I asked Wilson, after all of this Sturm und Drang, do knitters want to continue making Starmore's designs?

"Scarcity," she says. "Scarcity breeds desire. The yarn is no longer available. The book is no longer in print. You want stuff that is hard to get.

"There's the fact of the quality of the design. Her designs are beautiful. It is a badge of honor to be able to say, 'I have finished an Alice Starmore design.' You're talking about an entire Fair Isle garment. You're talking about advanced techniques that not everybody does," she concludes.

Wilson has never finished a Starmore, choosing instead to focus on her own designs, which have also become household names in the knitting world. Her Rogue, a cabled, hooded sweater, can be seen on at least one person in any crowd of knitters. Her soft cotton Shedir is a cabled chemo cap Wilson designed for Knitty.com's breast cancer awareness special issue.

"Not too long—maybe a few years—after I learned to knit, I discovered Starmore." Wilson saw *The Celtic Collection* and was "entranced by the Celtic-style cables. I bought that book. I started collecting the Alice Starmore books I could get my hands on because she is a wonderful designer. But I never actually got around to knitting anything of hers."

Then Wilson corrects herself. "I started a couple of the ones out of *Aran Knitting*. Later I started St. Brigid, and I actually got almost halfway through it. I definitely finished a back and I started a sleeve or something like that. But around the point when I got that far, I was getting disillusioned with the idea of making a big boxy sweater. Now I'm kind of wishing that I had finished it, but the shape of it—I didn't enjoy doing it. Also, by that point I'd also figured out that I hated having to follow other people's patterns, mainly because I had to keep going back and checking the chart to make sure I was following everything correctly. And if I was going to have to keep doing that, I'd rather it was my own design."

Starmore's Virtual Yarns, which she runs with her daughter Jade, does not mention any of these legal wrangles in the blog-style letters from Alice Starmore that are cataloged on the site.

I imagine Starmore as a ruddy, weatherbeaten woman who looks like Glenn Close in *Sarah, Plain and Tall*—but more

Scottish. And slightly more pit-bullish, since once she gets her teeth in something, there's no way she'll drop it.

While I admire her willingness to gear up for battle, she's not someone with whom I'd want to spend time. Like the reality of the Shetlands compared to their image, the Starmore who emerges isn't the delicate hand knitter out on her island but a hardened businesswoman who is thoroughly lawyered up. This doesn't stop me from wanting to knit her designs, however. That desire still burns as hotly as a thousand suns, although some practical problems may extinguish it.

3

April

The Discovery that Marjoram and Eucalyptus Are Not the Same Plant

Cost of 35 skeins of Shetland Spindrift: $169

I finished the hat.

In terms of demonstrating proof of concept, as Jenna Wilson and the Mythbusters say, it is a success. In terms of aesthetic appeal, well, you don't want to shield your eyes against the ugly, but it is not an object that inspires poetry. It will, however, keep your head warm.

Yes, it took three times as long as a hat usually takes me because I kept to my promise of holding the working yarn only in my left hand. I'm not about to focus on how long it took, because heartbreak lies down that path.

I did toss in three rows of two-handed colorwork in the middle, just to see if I could. The short answer is that I can. The longer answer is that it is a physical feat akin to walking backward on a treadmill. I can do that too, but it will never feel natural. My plans for the hat are simple: I will stick it in the great big pile of hats that lives in our coat closet. The next kid/husband who loses his or her chapeau will be forced to wear it as punishment.

It's time to get serious about Mary Tudor, however. Time is a-wasting.

The perfectionist knitter would be firmly impaled on the horns of a moral dilemma at this point. The yarns specified in the book—Alice Starmore's Campion line—are extremely difficult to get. Shops don't carry them. Starmore herself doesn't have them to sell and, frankly, given all the hoopla and hurt feelings, wouldn't anyway. A more dedicated knitter would shear her own sheep, spin her own yarn, and dye it. I don't have access to the original color cards for Campion, so figuring out the colors would be nearly impossible. I also don't have sheep. The perfectionist knitter, if she were being true to her craft, would spend years trolling eBay and picking up hanks of the yarn when it comes up in infrequent auctions.

That knitter would have to rely on luck, time, and deep pockets. Individual hanks, depending on the color, can go for upward of $30. Lots with multiple skeins of Campion can reach into the $300–$500 range. Given that Campion initially came in more than 130 colors, the odds are that you'd have no guarantee of ever getting in one box all the colors spec'ed for any given design. (A thrifty knitter could even reauction the colors she didn't need.)

I am not a perfectionist knitter. I'm also not sure I can handle the excitement of eBay bidding again. I could accidentally end up with a life-size replica of Stalin made out of cheese, simply because I couldn't stop clicking. Therefore, I take the easier route.

Jamieson's Shetland Spindrift is a near match for the Starmore yarn. Conversion charts that give you the Spindrift name for the Campion colors are easy to find with a Google search. Some names stay the same. Cobalt, Bracken, and Aubretia are a version of themselves. Oasis becomes Pistachio; Ginger is Yellow Ochre. The names alone are fabulous. I'll be working on a sweater that includes such evocative yarns as Loganberry and Cherry. If I get hungry, I can snack on it.

In my journal, I make a list. On one side are the Campion names; on the other, Spindrift. There's also some math involved. The discontinued yarns came in 150-yard hanks. Spindrift is in 115-yard skeins. It's easy enough to figure out. I do use a calculator just to be extra cautious.

Written in Tul blue ink, my chart looks like this:

Oasis 3 skeins (450 yrds total)	Pistachio 4 skeins (460 yrds)
Ginger 3 (450)	Yellow ochre 4 (460)
Cobalt 2 (300)	Cobalt 3 (345)
Delph 2 (300)	Cobalt 3 (345)
Bracken 2 (300)	Bracken 3 (345)
Aubretia 2 (300)	Aubretia 3 (345)
Damson 2 (300)	Loganberry 3 (345)
Violet 2 (300)	Purple 3 (345)
Thyme 2 (300)	Raspberry 3 (345)
Claret 1 (150)	Cherry 2 (230)
Marjoram 2 (300)	??????

Unfortunately, there are two Campion colors that don't have Spindrift near matches: Delph and Marjoram. The Delph problem can be easily solved. Cobalt, to my eyes, is close enough. While the idea of even suggesting I knit one of her designs with a "close-enough" match probably would have Starmore clawing at her hair in a fit of the howling fantods, I'm comfortable with this choice. And it is my sweater.

Marjoram, a yellowy gray green, proves to be a trickier wicket, as it turns out. There is no color that is close enough. I randomly pick a different green, Eucalyptus, from the Spindrift offerings and hope for the best.

My big box of yarn takes its own sweet time in getting to me. I'd ordered it from a Canadian online yarn shop, Camilla Valley Farms in Ontario, because they carry a staggering amount of Spindrift. The U.S. Customs folk must have decided that the box labeled "yarn" was a threat to our national security and sat on it for three weeks waiting to see if it would blow up. Or, in the customs office of my rich inner world, they were waiting to see if Mothra would hatch from it.

Yarn finally in hand, I fall into what can best be described as an anal-retentive fugue state. I photocopy all the Mary Tudor charts, one of which takes up a standard 8.5 × 11 inch page. I make my own gridlines, marking off every five rows and every five stitches. I put all the charts in individual sheet protectors. I label every skein with its corresponding chart symbol. I dump all the crap from my knitting bag and chuck all the stale gum, bent paper clips, crumpled sticky notes, and small plastic dinosaurs.

The small plastic dinosaurs were put there by my son and have nothing to do with knitting. It is, however, great fun to scatter big wads of yarn on the floor and stage a dinosaur tableau.

Thus prepared, I start my swatch, which is a simple, small square knitted with the yarn and needles you intend to use.

All knitting designers insist that swatches are a necessary evil. If you don't swatch, you are a bad knitter. You'll get the gout, they warn. Asteroids will crash into your backyard. Chaos will rule the land.

Designers, in short, like swatches.

Most knitters, in short, hate them. They keep you from diving right into your project, they whine. They are capital-B Boring.

But, the designers counter, without a swatch you don't know if you're getting the right number of stitches per inch (or centimeter, depending). You could use a lot more yarn than called for. Your garment won't fit.

Even though I know the designers are completely right, I'm not much of a swatcher. I don't bother doing them for small projects like mittens or scarves. Even medium-sized projects like kid's sweaters are swatch-free. But for something as intricate as Mary Tudor, I decide to suck it up. When faced with the idea of having to rip out and reknit any part of a Fair Isle pattern, I can be a grown-up.

The swatch is nearly my Waterloo. Five rows take thirty minutes. There are a total of forty-eight rows in the main pattern, which is what I'm swatching. So this piece of knitting, which will wind up being about ten by ten inches, will take about five hours. That is a long time for such a small piece of work. When I started the hat six weeks ago, that's when my yearlong countdown started. These five hours may be crucial to getting the whole project done on time.

I start to run the numbers. This pattern repeats around the body of the sweater eight times. If five rows of one repeat take thirty minutes, then five full trips around the sweater's body will take four hours. With forty-eight rows total per repeat, I might finish the stupid thing before my kids start college.

I decide that math is for suckers.

One reason, I reason, that I can take this stand is that I'm knitting the swatch flat. Go back to the previous image of the dot matrix printer. That's how this particular swatch needs to be made. It is an exceptionally silly way to knit Fair Isle, however, and I know that knitting it in the round, which is what I'll do once I start the actual project, will go much more quickly. Fair Isle done flat involves more dropping and picking up of colors than designers could ever intend. Fair Isle done in the round isn't nearly as fiddly and tedious because the color shifts line up better.

The other reason is that I'm slightly delusional most of the time, which makes niceties like accurate estimations of how time works a crapshoot.

Watching the pattern develop in the swatch is addictive. It honestly doesn't seem like these patterns of color stacked on top of each other should make anything but a nasty mess. And yet they add up to a unified whole, like a Seurat painting.

Because it is hard to stop knitting once the pattern grabs

you, no matter how challenging the two-handed technique still is, I finish the swatch in two days, instead of two weeks, which is what my hat experience had led me to expect.

I soak this small square of fabric in cool water for four hours in the bathroom sink. The goal with a wet block, which is what this is, is to let the wool fibers soak up as much water as they can, so that when it dries, the stitches will even themselves out. I'll do the same with the sweater, eventually, but will have to figure out another location for the soaking. The swatch barely fits in my bathroom sink.

You don't need to soak any piece of knitting for all that long, really. I simply forgot the swatch was in there.

You also need to be sure to use cold water for 100 percent wool yarns. If you need to know why, go watch the episode of *Laverne and Shirley* where Laverne washes Shirley's favorite sweater in hot water, then tosses it in the dryer. Warm water plus a little friction makes big wool things much smaller.

Once soaked, rolled into an old towel, and stomped on until the towel absorbs most of the water, the swatch is pinned onto my homemade, incredibly heavy blocking board, which my handy husband whipped up out of some plywood and Homasote. No, he's all mine. No, he doesn't have a brother.

While the swatch dries, a small discussion about knitters' jargon. Like any subculture worth its T-shirts, knitters have their insider lingo. All the yarn that you have packed away in closets, under beds, with the winter clothes, and in the freezer is called *stash*. Extreme stashers achieve a state called *SABLE*, which stands for "Stash Amassed Beyond Life Expectancy." Some are naturally low stashers. The Yarn Harlot claims that there is no such thing as a low stasher and that those who can fit all their yarn in one small bin are merely hampered by small houses or small budgets. Since I have both, I will concede her point.

KIP stands for "knitting in public" and is something we do to freak out the straights and make tedious lines at the DMV less so. *Frogging*, which doesn't involve amphibians, means pulling out large swaths of knitting at one go. You *rip it*. If you don't get the association, say it out loud. For smaller mistakes, you *tink* one stitch at a time. If you don't get that association, read *tink* backward.

One of the diseases that face knitters is *startitis*, which is the siren call of other projects when you are sick of the one that you are working on. This seems to rage epidemic-like in spring. For some, it is merely an acute phase that passes with a quick lie-down. For others, it is a chronic condition that results in bins full of needles with only a couple of rows of work on them.

The swatch, now dry, leads me to three conclusions.

The first is technical. I'll need to go up a needle size—from a U.S. 3 to a U.S. 4—to get the right number of stitches per inch. This is good to know.

The second is feline. Barney can't resist destroying wet wool that has been pinned down. Since we've had him for only a few months, which is a long story that isn't all that interesting, I didn't know that he is so angry about damp handknits. Attacking fabric is just odd. Straight pins stick out of the clawed-up but dry swatch like porcupine quills. I shake my fist and swear at him for a while. He simply stares at me.

The third problem is disheartening. Eucalyptus is not a substitute for Marjoram. It's not even close enough that you could squint your eyes and mumble, "It'll do." Eucalyptus leaps out of the design like a naked lady at a nun convention. So much so that my husband, when I show him the swatch, gently asks, "Before I say this, are you beyond the point where you could change anything?"

"Not at all," I say. "It's just a swatch. I was staving off gout."

"Anything you can do about that ugly green?"

"Get a different one." I explain that I was trying to find a substitute for a color that no longer exists.

"So you'll have to knit another swatch?"

"Theoretically," I say. If I were a perfectionist knitter, I would. But we've already established what kind of knitter I am.

The kind of knitter that I am right now is desperate. I troll the Ravelry Alice Starmore boards begging for information about Marjoram substitutes. Maybe there's a Spindrift shade that will work? Like Sage? Rosemary? There is no Thyme. I checked.

I'll pay, I exclaim. But no one can help this knitter out.

I email the Camilla Valley folks, who are very pleasant but admit that Marjoram is a tough color to match.

I flail around the Internet and stumble across She Ewe Knits, another Canadian online yarn shop. Canadians, it appears, love their Fair Isle. Their site mentions that they will make yarn packs for Starmore designs. I email Anne, the proprietress: "I'm trying to knit Starmore's Mary Tudor because, apparently, I had too much free time. Yes, I have the pattern. Yes, I've done the Campion-to-Spindrift substitutions. Except for the stupid Marjoram, which is about to drive me mad. If you have any suggestions, I'll gladly purchase them. Help."

You can almost feel the desperation.

Anne has no Marjoram to spare, sadly. She does sell complete Mary Tudor yarn packs but can't sell skeins individually. "It's a shade you can't replicate," she writes. "One that there isn't a close-enough shade out there for." But she'd be more than happy to hook me up with a complete yarn pack.

It turns out that I'm not desperate enough yet to pay for thirty-five more skeins of yarn.

Yet is the operative word.

I briefly flirt with the idea of spinning and dyeing my own Marjoram. I come up with a plan. First, I'll need to learn to spin. Then, I'll need to learn to dye. Then, I'll need to find a sample of what Marjoram actually looks like, because I can't even find a sample of it online. (In the too-little, too-late department: Jamieson added its own Marjoram to its color offerings about six months after I started my Mary Tudor.)

Even for me, this is a silly plan. I do what I always do when faced with a knitting crisis: I email Ann Shayne.

Ann is the southern half of the famous-in-knitter-circles Mason-Dixon team. She and her New York City–based cohort Kay Gardiner maintain a blog, have published two successful books, and have made a music video.

The song, called "Pardon Me, I Didn't Knit That for You," is an old-style country ballad about a case of mistaken identity, broken hearts, and, of course, knitting. Ann lives in Nashville, Tennessee, which means that there was no shortage of country music inspirations to draw from.

The costume choices for the video—big hair and melon-colored taffeta—tell you pretty much all you need to know about the Mason-Dixon approach to life. If that doesn't give it away, they ran an online contest inspired by *Project Runway*, where entrants had to knit up garments for taxidermied or otherwise stuffed animals; it was won by a toy monkey in an Oscar gown. In short, Ann and Kay take their amusements where they can.

A couple of years ago, I met Ann in person at the Southern Festival of Books in Memphis. She was promoting the first Mason-Dixon book, *The Curious Knitters' Guide: Stories, Patterns, Advice, Opinions, Questions, Answers, Jokes, and Pictures*. I was promoting my first book. I emailed her before the event to gush about my love of her blog and how it'd be swell to grab a beer at the convention hall.

One of the great features of the online knitter world is that it's rare to email a blogger and not get something back. There are exceptions, of course, but it is still a small-enough community that folks are genial. Ann is doubly so because she's from Nashville. That's my theory, anyway.

Long story short, the beer turned into a fun weekend about knitting, eating Mexican food, and thanking our collective stars that our readings were not slotted opposite Garrison Keillor's. Ann and I pinky-swore to come to each other's presentations so that at least one person would be there. She also pimped my reading at hers, which meant that my forty-five-minute chitchat about postpartum depression had a dozen women in it who were knitting away while I was talking.

Which is great, actually. If I could knit and talk, I'd do the same thing. One of the organizers asked me later, "What was with all of the knitters?" I wanted to tell him some fantastic story about a knitter bat signal that is shone on the full moon by a local yarn shop so that other knitters know one of their own is in the area. Instead, I shrug and say, "Ask Ann Shayne."

We've kept in touch since then. If she lived closer, it'd be fun to have her drop by for coffee and gossip. But Nashville to upstate New York is a long way to go for coffee and gossip, even very good coffee and very hot gossip. So we swap emails every now and again, usually about knitting or kids or the White Stripes. Religiously reading the blog, I noticed that she'd restarted her own Starmore project, a pullover called Keava. Ann was at a standstill, however, because she couldn't find any more Old Gold, a Campion color.

I did what any knitter would do, which is let her know that I felt her pain:

"Ann: Weird that you should have a Starmore Campion color kerfuffle. I'm working on my Mary Tudor swatch and I am ready to throw in the towel because the universe seems to have absorbed all of the Campion Marjoram and chucked it into a black hole. Oh, Alice. Why do you do this? My plan is to sub out a different green. But first I must wail and gnash my teeth. Might rend my garments too."

To which I got a reply:

"I have, like, a nauseating amount of Campion that I bought from a lady in Maryland years ago who was deaccessioning her collection. Like, a hundred or more skeins. Really sick!"

Lo and, indeed, behold, a few hours later, another email hit my in-box, this one with a picture of two hanks and one ball of Campion Marjoram. My whoop of joy startled Barney, who was sleeping in a sunbeam. Serves him right, swatch killer.

Faster than you can say, "I've always depended on the kindness of strangers," the yarn was in my mailbox. The manila envelope was decorated with Hatch Print Shop–style stamps featuring Ann and Kay's heads. The yarn had the old-school Alice Starmore tag, with a Celticesque leaf in a circle and the 100 percent pure Shetland wool trademark. "Marjoram 789," it read, "The Broad Bay Company. Fort Bragg, CA." I held it in my hands. It was perfect.

So perfect, in fact, that I had to hold it next to a ball of Jamieson's Spindrift. After that, I nearly sat right down and sobbed. The base yarns for the two are different. It might just be a color issue, since any given dye process can change the character of the yarn. But Campion Marjoram is a much less hairy yarn than Spindrift. The spin is tighter on the two plies, so much so that the Campion yarn is harder to break with your hands than the Spindrift. I know this because I got tired of searching for scissors while knitting the swatch and discovered that the yarn can be snapped with relative ease.

The Campion color is somehow more subtle and yet

deeper than the Spindrift, but again, that might just be how Marjoram is made. I don't have any other Spindrift shades that I can compare like to like against their Campion counterparts. Based on this realization alone, that these two yarns might not be as equivalent as I'd thought, I start to wonder what the hell I'm actually making. Once this sweater is done, will the substitutions I've made completely mess up the finished product?

I lie down for a little bit until the dizziness passes.

"I ran out of that color, the Old Gold," Ann says about why it took her so long to finish her own Starmore, Keava. We're sitting in her Nashville office, which is just off the foyer in her house. "I was going through all of the yarn, looking at all of those balls. It really was that I just needed one skein. I was like, 'Now that I'm looking for this yarn, I'm going to find it, even if it kills me.'"

Ann posted a bit on Mason-Dixon knitting about her Old Gold situation.

"This lady in New York emailed me and says, 'I have quite a bit,' which I find out is code for bales and bales of yarn, so much that you can't possibly . . . I mean, I have a box sitting out in the garage, I'll show you what 'I have quite a bit' means and how bad it is. She said, 'I'll send you all of my golds for you to see.' She sends me five different shades of gold, any of which would have done in a pinch. But there was one—there was a double skein of *the* gold, Old Gold. And it was incredible: she sent me all this yarn without a blink and understood what the problem was."

We're sitting in Ann's office because I want to talk to her about Starmore's designs and how they take over your life. I also just need a vacation and there are worse places to go than Nashville. Plus, I could write it off, so it was a double win. Ann, bless her, offered her guest room—more like guest wing—up to me. Her home is fabulous, very Southern chic with cool art on the walls. The prize-winning stuffed monkey graces the short dividing wall between kitchen and dining room.

Before I left, my husband said, "You're staying in the guest room of a person you barely know."

"Pretty much," I said. "I met her in person once. She sent me yarn."

"This is just something knitters do, isn't it?" he said.

"I think so. Besides, if she kills me and buries me in the backyard, she'll probably blog about it."

Knitters send you all of their golds too. Yarn in hand, Ann quickly finished up Keava, which she shows me. It's . . . different. Very late eighties with bright aquas, yellows, and pinks and crossed by lightning-inspired diagonals.

"See?" Ann says. "It's really quite ugly. It doesn't bother me, though. That's not really why I did it. It was just the making of it. It's really not even about the wearing of anything. It's a very peculiar impulse."

"Don't you usually knit things that you would wear?" I ask.

"I do want to wear the things I make," she says. "Some things I give away, but I do like making clothes. I went through a phase, especially when the first book came out, of making lots of blankies. That was fun.

"But when making a garment, you really have to aim. It can be a daunting task, sometimes. A dropped-shoulder sweater like Keava is not flattering at all and it never will be."

When it comes to adding sleeves to sweaters, options abound. A dropped shoulder is the simplest. You knit three rectangles—a big one for the body, two smaller and longer ones for the sleeves—then bung them all together at right angles. It's not the best idea to put a horizontal shoulder seam right across the upper arm because it makes that already troubling area look even more like an elephant's leg on some of us. But what it lacks in elegance, it makes up for in speed.

"Traditional Fair Isle sweaters are very clever. You can wear a lot of clothes under them. I was surprised when I wore Keava how light it is. It's not a heavy sweater," Ann says. "Those sheep—they've got it figured out."

"What I find satisfying is watching the pattern develop," I say.

"And then also there's those moments where you're knitting it and you're not really paying attention and you're still in the pattern. Love that. And then you screw up and you have to undo a row—but that's just part of it," Ann says, laughing.

Back when I was only knitting hats, when making each stitch felt like it needed 80 percent of my attention to complete, I'd laugh whenever other knitters would mention this flow state. Now I can churn out a straightforward hat while watching television without really noticing what my hands are doing. With stranded colorwork I still have to focus all my attention on each stitch, which kills any flow I could develop.

Still, I know what that flow state feels like from working as a writer. There are those elusive moments when you get lost in your work, when you'll lose all track of time and look up hours later and blink like a nocturnal beastie flushed from its hole. Those are the moments that you chase, since most of the time arranging words is as laborious as laying bricks. A writer's working conditions are better than a mason's, however.

My husband tells me that the same is true of golf. There are moments when it all aligns and your shot goes exactly where you want it. He also assures me that those rare moments are what keep you playing through all the times when your balls land in the sand and you stomp your hat in frustration.

I'm taking his word on the whole golf thing. With my Type A leanings, golf would be a pointless exercise in how quickly I could throw all the clubs into a water hazard. You cannot frog a putt.

For Ann, those moments when you get lost in the pattern are "like weeding. There is that meditative thing. It's quiet. It's pretty cause and effect. And your garden will be the better for it," she says, reaching for a pile of yarn ends on her desk, which are all the bits she snipped out while finishing Keava.

"I have a bag of those too," I said.

"What do you do with them? My friend Sheila puts them in the bushes for the birds. They make nests out of them," she says. I'm charmed by the idea of all Nashville's birds sitting in Easter-egg-colored nests.

"I learned to knit when I was in New York working in book publishing," Ann says. "I was trying to find a nonverbal activity because all I did all day was read bad manuscripts. Working in book publishing is very hard if you like to read, in my opinion. At least at the level I was, it was like working in the baloney factory—only you can eat baloney.

"I took a course at the Learning Annex. It was in the 1980s before there were all of these people knitting. I learned how to knit. I made a couple of sweaters, then I moved back to Nashville."

Like so many women, Ann rediscovered knitting when she had kids. And, like so many moms with kids, she took up the craft not because she wanted to clothe her kids but because she needed something to do with her hands.

"I guess the modern era of my knitting started when David was little, like four or so. My friend Franny was taking up knitting. We were waiting to go see Martha Stewart at the annual Antiques and Garden Show. All of Nashville was in line, waiting to see her. Apparently, all of the chairs in the auditorium had to be rearranged and we had to wait.

"In that line, Franny had her little ball of what I discovered later was Koigu, which is lovely. This little, delicious ball of yarn. She was making a tie for her husband, who is six seven, so it was really long. She said, 'Do you want to try?' And I said, 'Okay. Sure.' In a line that long, you've got to do something. She handed it to me and it was really like a light bulb: Oh. Yes.

"It was a time in my life where I had all of these little periods of chopped-up waiting. With little kids, there's just a lot of waiting. You can't read. You can't sustain five minutes of attention. But knitting was great. Then I really got the bug."

At first Ann started with small projects but soon needed more of a challenge to stay interested.

"I knit stuff for David, baby stuff. I knit Fair Isle flat, which was one of the stupidest things I ever did. It was just the most punishing thing you'll ever do. There's a reason you do it in the round. It really works. It's the only way.

"The thing about knitting is that it can always be infinitely harder. You bite off what you think you can handle and make your way through that. Usually, you succeed at it because you usually aim low enough. A lot of times, I think people are less adventuresome than they could be. Once you make a sweater and the sleeves don't fall off, it's so exciting.

"The first sweater I made had a button band, and there were buttons I sewed onto it and the buttons went through the holes. People who saw it were like 'That's the cutest thing I've ever seen.' And your response is 'Thanks. It is,'" Ann says, as she looks down at the floor modestly.

Ann and I start talking about hard projects. The definition of *hard* differs for every knitter. For me, projects that require counting are hard, since I seem to have a knack for losing track of stitches or randomly adding them, sometimes in the same row.

For Ann, her hardest project was a lace shawl called Birch, designed by Rowan. Birch is knitted from Kidsilk Haze, a yarn jokingly called Cracksilk Haze because if you work with it once, you'll crave it for life.

Kidsilk Haze is a gorgeous yarn, no doubt. The colors are rich—and richly named: Trance, Anthracite, Blood, Splendour. It's a silk-mohair blend spun into a light, lacy yarn. The only problem with Kidsilk Haze is that it is nearly impossible to rip stitches out if you make a mistake because the mohair acts like a sticky fiber superglue when it comes into contact with itself. Given that it's frequently easier to simply toss the whole project out rather than rip-and-reuse the yarn, there has been idle speculation (by me, anyway) that this is a design feature not a flaw. Just think of how much extra yarn Rowan can sell to easily distracted knitters.

"All of a sudden I looked up and my little leaf isn't looking like a leaf. And I don't know why that happened," Ann says. "Overcoming that frustration was hard. With that shawl, you start with three hundred stitches. I wasn't afraid of casting on, it's just boring. But it does mean if you screw up, it's pretty punishing to get back."

With most yarns, if you drop a stitch while slipping it from your left needle to your right needle, you can immediately see the horrifying result because that column of stitches will unravel in front of your disbelieving eyes. With sticky Kidsilk Haze, a dropped stitch won't unravel. As Ann puts it, "It will just sit there politely for hours, even days," which means that you may be dozens of rows past the mistake before you even notice that you've made one.

One way to keep from making these mistakes is to put a stitch marker, which can be anything from a small rubber band to a handmade crystal pendant, to mark each pattern repeat. If you end up with the wrong number of stitches in each repeat, you immediately know that you've screwed up.

"I had to start over three times. By the third time, I'm like, 'I'm putting a marker every ten stitches, every repeat.' That felt like a real failure. I can't believe I had to do that. But that was the only way I could really get it. Psychologically, it's helpful to know there's a limit to how awful the mistake can be," Ann says.

Since we're talking about our first knitted lace projects, I mention making an Icarus shawl as a wedding gift for a friend, who was going to wear it with her gown. Rather than take the sensible approach—the one where you place markers at every pattern repeat—I decided to wing it. As the wedding day approached, I knit faster and faster. Somewhere I screwed up, but there was no time to fix it. I wasn't certain that a nonknitter would be able to pick out where it all went wrong, but I knew a knitter would itch to fix it. And the bride was a knitter.

When I gave it to her, I mumbled something about the Amish philosophy of making sure there was a small mistake in every handmade item, since only the Divine can create something perfectly formed. Or maybe that was the Shakers, I added. Or Middle Eastern rug weavers. Actually, I said, forget that example. While I aim for perfection, I rely on my uncanny ability to screw it up somewhere along the line first. So I don't have to purposely add errors.

No, I said, like marriage, this shawl is imperfect. Ultimately, you hope that the flaws don't distract from the object's intention and beauty.

Which is a sentiment I wholeheartedly feel. Still, I wish my Icarus had been perfect, and I wanted to make another one just to prove that I could.

Ann has similar feelings.

"The thing about Birch that really got me is that once I'd made it, I really wanted to make another one. But I really didn't feel the need to own it," she says. "When I first started knitting, I was very possessive of every stitch. I hated picking out errors. It was such an achievement to just make anything. Once I made that shawl, I realized 'I can do this.'

"I've given away more shawls than I've kept. I don't really feel the need to keep them anymore."

Ann is currently working on another Starmore. This sweater is called Donegal and is a murky blend of colors overlaid with curvy lines. While Keava is in too many bad bridesmaid dress shades for my tastes, Donegal is absolutely stunning.

I also find it stunning that Ann is working on it during a Nashville June, where the temps frequently rise into the eighties and the humidity makes the air feel like a hot sponge.

"I think it's harder to be a southern knitter," I say.

"It is a challenge," Ann says. "I had an email from a friend yesterday who said, 'I can't read about Donegal right now. It makes me too hot. I really am sorry.'

"I've always loved the pattern. That was one of the books that came when Kay and I bought a giant box of yarn on eBay. The curviness of the pattern goes counter to what Fair Isle normally looks like.

"I was worried that the repeat was so wide it would just be a total chore. You know how you work out the shorthand on the rows, counting stitches to yourself—three, two, one, one? That really works for doing Fair Isle. It's always one color or the other. Just make sure you're using the right color at the beginning of the row. There's totally a rhythm to it. Even a fairly long repeat like that is manageable.

"There are many appeals of Fair Isle. It's something that looks hard. There's something very satisfying about it. There's the rhythm to it, once you get the hang of it. Watching the pattern come alive—I don't understand why that's so addicting. With Fair Isle, I get the feeling of connection with something that's very old and very traditional. I really do think about the people who did it on those little islands."

In the moments when the knitting—any knitting, not just Fair Isle—is going well, that connection is easy to feel. Despite our modern methods of pooling knowledge and updating designs, the craft itself remains the same. There are only a few ways to make a knit stitch. There are only a few ways to purl. Women—and some men, to be fair—have been making hats, scarves, and sweaters this same way for hundreds of years. They've also constantly come up with new ways to keep the same old work engaging. The Fair Islanders did it with color.

"The yarn part's fun in Fair Isle, part of the puzzle of it. I'm really just starting to get into all of that. The colors in the background and the foreground are always changing.

"I just like the dark colors," she says. "You really have to work at it in good light. I was knitting in Boston; I was doing it at a skatepark in bright sunlight and I was like, 'This thing is very loud.' But it takes bright sunlight to make it loud."

"With a lot of Starmore patterns," I add, "the yarns aren't easy to get. Here's what I'm trying to figure out: if you knit a Starmore sweater but don't use the yarns, do you still have a Starmore sweater?"

"That's a question a lot of designers have, especially now when there's been such a proliferation of patterns. You see designers doing shortcuts that you recognize involving stitch dictionaries and adapting a basic pattern. There are certain books, like Ann Budd's, that give a template that you see used a lot. It gets kind of tricky when it's a pattern that's not very distinctive or that doesn't have something really surprising in it."

When it comes to functional handknit garments, in other words, it's hard to come up with something truly new. A sweater, to fully earn the name, needs to have two sleeves and a body. Any number of pattern books lay out templates that tell you how to knit something in a sweater shape. A designer can then treat that template like the outlines in a coloring book and fill in the shape with a pattern of his or her own choosing.

Every now and again, however, a designer will come along and blow the old models to bits, like Henry Ford did with the assembly line. Ford took a fixed result and figured out a new way to do it. You can argue about the positive or negative repercussions the invention of the assembly line had, certainly. But you'd still have to admit that it has changed the process of building cars forever.

Currently, the knitting equivalent of Henry Ford is Cat Bordhi, whose new approaches to sock knitting have had a ripple effect in the larger knitting world. While her new technique will still result in a sock, the way she gets there is unlike any that the knitting world has seen before.

The simplest sock is a tube that is closed at one end. But as children who were forced to wear them in the seventies can attest, straight tube socks aren't comfortable. The fabric bunches under the arch of your foot and cuts into your skin where it's forced to stretch over your heel.

Tailored socks—the socks that look like a foot when you hold them up—are more comfortable. Around your arch, the sock is gusseted, so that it grows wider as it approaches your ankle. Some ease is built into the heel so that the fabric better follows the shape of the foot and, as a result, lasts longer.

Knitters take these innovations one step further by measuring their own feet and shifting these elements around until the sock is bespoke. What Bordhi has done is take all of these elements and changed where they start and stop. For example, the gussets that lead up to the heel don't have to stay on the sides of the foot. Instead, you can move them around, which opens up more possibilities for patterns and shapes. The genius part is that once you wrap your mind around the technique, it is endlessly mutable. You don't just know how to knit one particular sock; you now have a new way to think about all socks.

Ann thinks that Starmore can be cited as another innovative knitter. The difference between Starmore and Bordhi is that Starmore offers a new way to think about color rather than architecture.

Before Starmore, Fair Isle sweater motifs were traditional. There were OXOs, that is, a repetition several rows high of those characters. The OXO evolved not because the islanders loved oxen; instead, that pattern kept the yarn floats on the back short enough not to get caught by your fingers every time you put your sweater on. *Peeries* also show up in most traditional patterns. A peerie is any small—four or five stitches long by up to seven rows deep—pattern that repeats over a row. Peeries frequently look like little diamonds or oblongs.

These old-school Fair Isles were knitted from bright, almost garish color combinations. Dialing down the dyeing process to create more subtle colors was harder to do before chemical dyes were perfected. Just look at the difference between photographs taken in the early 1960s and now.

Geography was also responsible for those loud colors. Imagine what it must be like to live in a mostly brown and green place. And think about how much easier it is to see your husband wandering across the windswept heath when he is swathed in cherry red and chartreuse?

While Starmore didn't do much to modify the dropped shoulder shape of a sweater, she did revolutionize what patterns were on it and which colors were used. Peeries and OXOs show up every now and again, but they are not a staple in her designs. Instead, she'll use crowns, flowers, and fleurs-de-lis, like she does in the Mary Tudor design. Or Celtic-flavored spirals, which are the central motif in the Donegal pattern.

Starmore also manipulated the colors according to their values, a statement that requires a quick dip into color theory to visualize. If you have a yarn stash, head to it now and sit in front of it. If your yarn stash takes up more than one room, grab all the skeins of one color that you can find and dump them in a pile. If you have no stash, find something that you have a lot of, like crayons or fat quarters or cats. For instance, I have a coffee mug full of blue pens, each of which is from a different manufacturer and, therefore, a different blue.

Now imagine a long, skinny rectangle with white at one end and black at the other. In between are grays. From the white side is a gray with one drop of black, then two drops of black, then three drops of black, and onward until it is all black. Now arrange all your yellow yarns (or blue pens or brown cats) according to that scale. Put the yellow with the most white at one end, then progress incrementally until you get to the yellow with the most black. You've now arranged that color by its *value*.

If you put your whitest yellow yarn next to your blackest yellow yarn, the result is called *high contrast*. The yellows that wind up next to each other on this scale are, sensibly, *low contrast*. If you do this for all your yarns, from the purples to the greens to the reds, the hues that fall in the same place on this scale—for example, all the yarns that are closest to the main color plus two drops of black—are low contrast when put next to each other. Rather than put two high-contrast tones next to each other, one of Starmore's gifts is finding two colors that shouldn't work together, like dusky purple and pea soup green, and making them harmonize by using hues of the same value.

Ann decided to knit her Donegal completely out of the big boxes of Campion yarn in her garage. Even if she didn't have the exact color Starmore called for, Ann was determined to find one that was close, a feat made easier because she also owns Starmore shade cards.

She pulls out the swatch she made with the colors from her Campion stash that she thought might work. It's nice but doesn't have that same zing that Starmore designs have. Then she pulls out her Donegal in progress, which uses the exact colors Starmore chose.

The difference is striking. From a distance, even under the strong Nashville sun, the colors almost dance off each other, even though they all appear to be similar drab tones of gray and blue. Up close, you can see the bubble gum pink and the mossy green and dozen other yarns that give the design depth and life.

"I find it completely fascinating," Ann says. "It's very humbling. I thought I was doing so great with yarns from my stash. I thought 'this was really something.' But I really didn't like how it looked. It's really hard to do this well. Having done this, I now recognize her skill and have a lot of respect for it. I have a whole different understanding of how to do it. You have to choose really carefully. The color matters a lot."

"So if you had swapped out the colors, would you still have a Starmore at the end?" I ask.

"I think working on this sweater makes me realize that her particular yarns and her particular patterns create something that is uniquely hers," Ann says. "If you swap out the yarn, it does turn into something different. I understand why she's so careful about protecting that."

With most other knitting projects, the knitter has more

control over the knitted object's destiny. You choose the type and color of the yarn. You fiddle with the gauge, if you want, and the sizing. Don't like a dropped shoulder? Fine. Design a new one that you like better. It just takes a little bit of math and a lot of patience because you'll probably screw it up the first time.

But Starmore's colors and patterns are so precise that they can't be monkeyed around with too much before their magic evaporates. At a certain point, you have to trust her eye. While bubble gum pink and mossy green look like a biology experiment gone horribly wrong, in the sweater, they are stunning. But you have to cede control to Starmore.

"Our first book," Ann says, "had a lot of stuff in there that left a huge amount of latitude. It's been really interesting watching how people use that idea and what they come up with. To us, the projects are just a concept, a technique. It's not a set of patterns. It's a way to make a blanket. How you choose to configure your squares is up to you.

"The results vary wildly, and we love that. We think everybody has a little bit of genius somewhere—or should just experiment with it. If they discover that it looks like a pile of crap, then maybe they should find a more rigid pattern.

"I think most garments that I see in patterns can sustain being done in a lot of different yarns. But at what point does it stop being that pattern?" she asks. "It's a very good question. It's something that every designer puzzles over."

On that last thought, we decide to break for a bit of yarn shopping at the puzzlingly named Germanic Haus of Yarn, which is a lot like the bar in Cheers. Everyone knows Ann's name. No beer, though. With the name, you'd think there ought to be beer and schnitzels.

I fall in love with a skein of Colinette Jitterbug (a Welsh yarn) in a "colourway" called Copperbeech. I have no plans for it but can't resist its siren call. Besides, yarn is the perfect souvenir.

4

May

Embracing the Body While Ignoring the Fact of Arms

3 pairs U.S. size 4 Addi Turbo circular needles (one of which I never use because it's not slippery enough) in 16" and 40" lengths, plus 1 set U.S. size 4 double-pointed bamboo needles and 1 set U.S. size 3 double-pointed bamboo needles: $56

Mary Tudor begins with casting on 357 stitches in Cobalt. Normally, I would not identify myself as someone who is unable to count to 357. I can get all the way up into the thousands before I have to keep track on a spare sheet of paper.

I'm using a circular needle, which has two metal points on the ends connected by a length of very narrow plastic tubing. If you hold the two ends together, the needles form a circle and are perfect for knitting long tubes. Just as horses prefer certain styles of saddles, knitters develop preferences for certain types of needles. I used to swear by bamboo for everything but now only use wood for socks and sleeves. I've tried plastic, parti-colored aluminum, and casein. While there are glass needles, I've never used them because their beauty distracts me from the knitting at hand. In the past, needles used to be made from tortoiseshell, ivory, and bone, a practice that has, thankfully, died out.

I prefer the fantastically expensive, for knitting needles, Addi Turbos. The tips are nickel-plated brass that a sticky Shetland wool yarn like Jamieson's slides easily around. Addis are not the ne plus ultra of needles. That honor belongs to the ones being made by Signature Needle Arts, a company founded by Cathy Bothe, a knitter who happened to also work for a metal fabrication company that makes surgical equipment. Their precision-milled double-point sets start at forty-five dollars. I'm told that the knitting experience is like moving from a Yugo to a BMW. One day, maybe, I'll break down and test-drive them. My fear is that I'll never be able to go back.

Double-pointed needles, which I'll use for the sleeves, are the oldest known knitting needles, according to Richard Rutt's *A History of Handknitting*. Knitting starts to show up in paintings around the fourteenth century, and the women pictured are using wooden double-pointed needles.

Unless forced, I won't use straight needles, which have a point on one end and a knobby thing at the other to keep the stitches from falling off. This has more to do with thrift, even though knitting with straights makes me feel like I'm rowing with very ineffective oars. Most of my needle inventory is of the circular sort because they can also be used for flat knitting.

No matter how much you may want to, you can't knit a tube with straight needles.

As for the size issue, bigger isn't always better. The diameter of the needle needs to work with the gauge of the yarn and the technique of the knitter in order to produce a pleasing fabric. As for the numbers themselves, a U.S. size 4 is different from a UK/Canadian size 4, which is different again from a Japanese size 4. The industry is slowly going metric, which means my U.S. 4 is 3.5 mm in diameter.

The act of knitting is like a fingerprint. Some knitters are habitually loose, which means they have to go down a needle size or three to get the right fabric. Some are tight, which means they need to go up. Figuring this out is one of the reasons designers suggest knitting a swatch. They also suggest the swatch because they are closet sadists.

I may be projecting.

Needles in hand, I cast on 357 stitches. I count again—359. No problem. I rip two stitches out. Count again—356. Cast on another—356. Again. Crap. Pull needle out of work and unravel all of it, because my counting mojo is not on my side. Steps must be taken.

Cast on 100 stitches and place marker. Cast on 100 more and place marker. Ditto 100 more. Count stitches—302. Roll eyes up to heavens. Pull needle out of work and unravel.

Cast on 50 stitches and place marker. Count those stitches again to make sure there are still just 50. Cast on 50 more and place marker. Count all of them to make sure the total's still 100. Do this until you reach 350 stitches. Count again and get 349.

Mutter impolite words under your breath. Think about taking up different hobby. Skeet shooting's fun, I hear.

Cast on 20 stitches and place marker. Recount. Cast on 20 more. Recount. Do this until you reach 340. Count and get 340. Count again and still get 340. Ponder loud whoop of joy but hold back out of fear of waking the children.

Cast on 17 more stitches. Count and get 357. Count again. Still 357. Consider reinvestigating previous stance on religion just so that you have a deity to thank.

I look at the clock and realize hours have passed, which explains, at least, why I need to pee. I give up and go to bed.

Starmore's Tudor Roses patterns are all united, naturally, by a Tudor dynasty theme. Even the book's title has a historical element. Henry VII was the Tudor king who ended the bitter war between the houses of York and Lancaster after Richard III's death in battle. York's supporters always wore a badge with a white rose; Lancaster's always wore red during the War of the Roses, which wasn't just a movie with Michael Douglas and Kathleen Turner. When Henry Tudor was crowned Henry VII, he designed an emblem that combined both roses, called the Tudor Rose.

In Starmore's *Tudor Roses*, there are sweaters for men in honor of Henrys VII and VIII, and sweaters for women inspired by Mary and Margaret Tudor, Catherine of Aragon (who gets both a cardigan and a tunic), Elizabeth I, and all of Henry's wives. Jade Starmore, Alice's daughter, designed Aragon, Anne Boleyn, Anne of Cleves, and Catherine Howard. Six of the patterns feature complicated cables; seven feature equally complicated Fair Isle. Starmore relates the patterns on each to the person honored. Anne Boleyn's, for example, features a falcon, as hawking was her favorite hobby.

(Henry and his wives appear to be rich fodder for at least one more knitter. Katie Park—also known as Caffaknitted in the online craft networks at etsy.com and ravelry.com—in Boone, North Carolina, designed knitted doll versions of the man and the six women, two of which were beheadable. My favorite is Catherine Howard, if only for her removable head and the violet in her hair.)

Alice Starmore's obsessive attention to every detail is truly breathtaking. The photos in *Tudor Roses* were shot at Hever Castle, which was Anne Boleyn's family's home until Henry VIII snatched it as part of her dowry, then gave it to Anne of Cleves as part of their divorce settlement. Also included are Alice's notes about the Tudors, descriptions of the castle, a helpful chart of the lineage, and essays describing the design choices for each sweater.

Even Alice herself admits that the bulk of the designs in *Tudor Roses* are a step beyond what sane people would ordinarily attempt. In her introduction, she says that some "require diligence and skill" and involve "complex knitting mathematics." To which I say, "No shit, Alice."

Given that I am an American, which means that I can name all the kids on *The Brady Bunch* but can't recite the kings and queens of England, I initially think Mary Tudor and Mary, Queen of Scots are the same person. In my own defense, I can sing the Preamble to the Constitution, thanks to *Schoolhouse Rock*, and can name all the states and their capitals, thanks to Miss Stoehr, my fifth-grade teacher. I also can tell you in rhyme how each of Henry VIII's wives got booted out of the queenhood: "divorced, beheaded, died; divorced, beheaded, survived."

Mary, Queen of Scots, as it turns out, wasn't a Tudor at all, which explains the lack of a Starmore sweater named after her. M,QoS was a Stuart eventually executed for plotting to kill Queen Elizabeth I, who was Henry's daughter with his second wife, Anne Boleyn. Mary Tudor was Henry's youngest sister, who would briefly be the queen of France. His other sister, Margaret, was M,QoS's grandmother. There is another Mary Tudor, of course (because why should this be easy?), who becomes known as Bloody Mary. We'll get to her in a minute.

The whole keeping track of British royalty thing would be much easier if they weren't all named Henry, Mary, or Elizabeth, with the occasional Charles chucked in to break the monotony. The Brits would also help their cause if their retellings of history didn't play fast and loose with what actually happened.

Yes, I'm talking about *The Tudors*, the Showtime series. I Netflixed it in the hopes that it would bring me up to speed on how all the folks Starmore designed sweaters for were related. My lazy way out would have worked if the series' creators hadn't decided to combine Mary and Margaret Tudor into one character—Margaret—who was lustily played by the gorgeous Gabrielle Anwar. According to writer and creator

Michael Hirst, "I didn't want two Princess Marys on the call sheet, because it might have confused the crew." Yes, because confusing the crew would be more unfortunate than confusing the viewers, who could totally handle two characters named Mary.

The other Mary Tudor, Princess Mary, was the one who became known as Bloody Mary. She was Henry VIII's daughter by Catherine of Aragon, his first wife. This Mary would briefly be queen of England and earn her sobriquet by being a devout Catholic who put to death a couple of hundred Protestants by having them burned at the stake. Another fun fact to know and trade is that Mary I had two false pregnancies, which later turned out to be a stomach tumor, and died without producing an heir. She has no Tudor Roses sweater, which is too bad, because the design possibilities are amusingly grim.

Henry, Margaret, and the first Mary were the only three of Henry VII's seven children to live long enough to reproduce. Three of Henry VII's seven children didn't even make it to age four, which makes me pause for a minute and thank van Leeuwenhoek for his pioneering work on microscopes and contributions to germ theory. I am privileged to live in a time and place where I can assume that my kids will make it to adulthood. I can't imagine what it must be like to lose half your babies before they even hit the age of reason.

Arthur, the oldest of Henry VII's kids and presumptive heir, died at age fifteen (or sixteen, depending on your source), shortly after marrying Henry VIII's future bride, Catherine of Aragon. When Henry later wants to divorce his Spanish Katie to get into Anne Boleyn's skirts, he uses that fraternal history to justify his actions, but that's a different story. *The Tudors* tells that part of the Tudor saga successfully, even if I find it hard to watch because of the historical gaffes and because Jonathan Rhys Meyers reminds me of a creepy boy I made out with in high school. Which is also a different story.

Mary Tudor was a stunner in her day. In *Henry VIII: The King and Court*, Alison Weir quotes the philosopher Erasmus on Mary T that "Nature has never formed anything more beautiful." Mary was also a hit at social functions, according to historian Maria Perry in her 1998 book *The Sisters of Henry VIII*. "Mary . . . was (judging from the number of pairs of shoes she wore out) lively and physically active from an early age. She was later to become an accomplished dancer, playing a leading part in court masques."

Perry points out that Mary was the one in the family with the sharpest sense of humor, which makes her the princess after my own heart. In her letters, "the phrase 'I marvel much,' which she may have picked up from her grandmother, indicates that she is standing on her dignity and some gem of sarcastic observation usually follows." I've made a mental note to work "I marvel much" into my own correspondence. It also appears that Mary, unlike the rest of the red-haired Tudors, was blond.

When Mary was eighteen, she was married off to fifty-two-year-old King Louis XII of France, a union that she vehemently opposed, perhaps because the king was "feeble and pocky," according to historical accounts. Mary's bad attitude aside, she sucked it up for her country and married the sickly Louis.

Mary's beauty won the hearts of most of the folks she encountered. The Venetian ambassador to Louis' court called Mary "a paradise." When after Louis' death she attended the Field of the Cloth of Gold, an extravagant diplomatic meeting between Henry and France's King François I near Calais, a French officer said, "Madame, you are the rose of Christendom. You should have stayed in France. We would have appreciated you."

Happily for her, three months into the marriage, Louis died, allegedly from overexerting himself in the royal bedchambers. By his own account, on his wedding night alone, he'd "crossed the river three times." The French court kept Mary around for a few weeks after Louis' death, just to see if she was pregnant with an heir. Then they consented to send her back to England at her request, and François I took the throne.

Her behavior on returning to England created a tabloid-worthy scandal or, given the period, a ballad-worthy one. Quoting from *Mary Tudor: The White Queen* by Walter C. Richardson:

Eighth Henry ruling this land,
He had a sister fair,
That was the widow'd Queen of France,
Enrich'd with virtues rare;
And being come to England's Court,
She oft beheld a knight,

Charles Brandon nam'd, in whose fair eyes,
She chiefly took delight.

The Tudors would have you believe that Henry promised his sister the right to marry for love after she had married for political convenience. Historians suspect there's more romance than truth to this claim, even though it does make for a good story and makes Henry a sympathetic royal. Still, Mary Tudor pulled off a love match under Henry's nose, even though it almost got her and her betrothed sent to the chopping block.

After Louis' death, Henry had sent his buddy, Charles Brandon, the first duke of Suffolk, to France to retrieve Mary. Brandon swore that he had no designs on the king's sister, whom he knew from court. Swept away by love (or lust) before their trip across the Channel, Brandon and Mary Tudor married in secret with King François' aid. When news got back to the English court, the couple was accused of treason and threatened with beheadings. Eventually, Cardinal Wolsey talked Henry out of his murderous rage and the Brandons were merely fined, rather than executed.

There's another aspect to the king's willingness to allow this match that has nothing to do with Wolsey's silver tongue. While she was the French queen, Mary was given fabulous jewelry by her adoring husband, including the Miroir de Naples, a diamond valued at 60,000 crowns. It's not hard to imagine that Henry wanted to add all these riches to his royal coffer, and so his anger may have been more for show than for spite. Regardless, most of Mary's booty, including the Miroir de Naples, paid the fine that Henry levied.

In the midst of her brother's threats of punishment, Mary threatened to retire to a nunnery if Henry didn't let her make the match she wanted. In the convent, she wrote, "never no man shall joy of me." Mary keenly knew her true value as both a political chess piece and a source of income for the crown. For Henry, it was better to have her married to an ally, even if he wasn't a high-status one. Henry, perhaps after eyeing Mary's jewels again, capitulated. Clearly, the Tudor spunk—the same streak that led to the reigns of both Bloody Mary and Elizabeth I—was bright in Henry's sister as well.

Brandon and Mary became the progenitors of the Suffolk line of Tudors: Henry (yes, another Henry); Frances, who would be the mother of Lady Jane Grey (who would after Henry VIII's death be queen for nine days before being beheaded by Bloody Mary); and Eleanor. After Mary's death in 1533, Brandon quickly remarried. His new bride was both his fourteen-year-old ward and his dead son's fiancée.

The sweater that Starmore designed lives up to this colorful history. Bright blue and a brighter red are the main hues, and they are set off by golds and green. Like Mary Tudor herself, the end product is not subtle. Palm-sized fleurs-de-lis alternate with equally large Tudor roses, a motif that looks like an open rose nestled inside another open rose. Knitted crowns separate these elements. Starmore's version of the Tudor rose is stylized, but it is clear what this pattern represents.

It's a design that shouldn't work because, to quote the fabulous Tim Gunn, visionary fashion critic, "It's a lot of look."

But rather than overwhelm, it enchants. Like the woman who inspired it, it is a paradise.

The first round of knitting Mary Tudor, contrary to what I'd expected, isn't too bad. Fair Isle colorwork is a completely binary process. Each row uses only two colors. As long as you start that round with the right one, following the pattern isn't rocket science. Ann's method of chanting the numbers helps. In my head I hear two yellow, two blue, two yellow, five blue, one yellow, six blue, seven yellow, six blue, one yellow, five blue, two yellow, two blue, one yellow. Even the two-handed knitting technique is going okay.

The work is not speeding right by, but it's not as bad as I'd feared. Twelve rounds in, which measures two inches at best, and I can see the pattern lining up. It's like playing Tetris, which was one of my weaknesses during college. Fitting those blocks together must feed in to my love of order. Watching this pattern develop must nourish the same impulse. Out of nothing but string, I'm making something beautiful.

My one concession to my own inability to count reliably are the stitch markers I've placed at the end of every pattern repeat. There are eight repeats of the pattern per complete round. If I reach the marker at the end of one repeat and have too many or too few stitches or that stitch is the wrong color, I only have to rip out, at most, forty-two stitches. And the Douglas Adams fan in me loves the symbolism of that number.

I'd like to say that this marker technique is an innovation

that has sprung forth from my brain like Athena from Zeus's. Instead, I have to give credit to the Internet. In 2004 the Craft Yarn Council estimated that there were 53 million American women who knew how to knit. As the Craft Yarn Council also likes to remind us, a few of those women are celebrities like Julia Roberts, Vanna White, Sarah Jessica Parker, and Hilary Swank.

If you've ever wondered where most of those knitters are, you aren't looking online. A simple Google search for "knitting blog" brings up 1 million hits. By way of comparison, "needlepoint blog" gets you 335,00 possibilities, "woodworking blog" yields 533,000, and "scherenschnitte blog" (it's a German papercutting craft) produces 22,300 hits.

Ravelry.com, a Facebook-like place for knitters to meet, talk yarn, and get advice, has 500,000 users (as of November 2009) and 1,500 more join each day. In 2007, 65 percent of knitters under the age of thirty-five were likely to turn to the Internet for knitting guidance.

It's not just U.S. knitters who use the Internet to connect with other knitters. Stephanie Pearl-McPhee, the Yarn Harlot, had the top-ranked blog in Canada in 2008. Not the top-ranked knitting blog, mind. Her blog trounced blogs about politics, sports, and music. The question isn't "Are knitters online?" It's more useful to ask, "Why are knitters online?"

The question can be partly answered by looking at knitting culture's demographic shift. According to *American Demographics* magazine, "What is perhaps even more significant than the fact that, by attracting additional participants in recent years, knitting has bucked the trend is that knitters today tend to be younger, better educated, and wealthier than they were in 1999. MRI [Mediamart Research, Inc.] reports that the average knitter in 2002 was 55.7 years old, while knitters three years before that were 56.8 years old, on average—quite a feat, considering that the population of the United States as a whole is aging."

The same research goes on to state that 31 percent of knitters have a bachelor's degree or beyond, compared to 26 percent in 1999. More education leads to more income too. The average knitter earned $39,000 a year in 2002, which leaves her nearly $8,000 more for yarn than in 1999.

A younger median age, greater education, and higher income suggest a population that is more comfortable with the online world. Most of these women are adept at using computers already, since most of these women are young enough to have worked at jobs that require knowing how to navigate a Windows platform.

In *Vogue Knitting*'s twenty-fifth anniversary issue, writer Cheryl Krementz asked what has caused knitting to take such a hold in our culture during the last ten years.

"The Internet," answered Vickie Howell, host of DIY Network's *Knitty Gritty*.

"It's the Internet," answered *Knitter's Review*'s Clara Parkes.

"I don't think it was the Internet," answered McPhee. "I'd say it was the socialization of knitting. Taking knitting from a solitary activity into something we do out in our communities and form our own communities around. And I think the Internet was a catalyst for that—a lot of things were. But one of the reasons this industry's got such great legs is that people aren't just knitting; they're forming communities, and communities are harder to walk away from than knitting projects. I've walked away from thousands of knitting projects."

If not for the Internet and the online knitting community, I wouldn't still be knitting today. While I did learn a few of the basics as a kid, I'd completely forgotten them by the time I was ready to try again. I didn't know any knitters in person. I didn't feel comfortable walking into a yarn shop and asking for that much of their time. But I had no problem with surfing for a demonstration online, which I could watch as many times as it took for me to understand. (It took much longer than I'd care to admit.)

When I was a new mom knitting baskets of hats and fending off extreme isolation, the knitting blogosphere was a lifesaver. Every day I'd check the blogs of my friends on the computer, just to see what they were up to. Each of these women—and almost all of them were women—showed me more techniques, yarns, and patterns than I'd ever dreamed were out there.

I still read all those blogs, not because I'm lonely but because those writers feel like my friends, even though I'd wager most of them have no idea that I'm out here. I have a sense of what they've been through in their lives, how they dealt with it, and what they knitted along the way.

Eventually, a language will come up with a word for blog friends. I suspect that the Germans—given their love of smooshing a couple nouns together to get one big word that captures all the nuances of an emotional state—will be the ones to coin it.

Susette Newberry, an outreach coordinator/reference librarian in Ithaca, NY, gives me inspiration on the days when counting to forty-two is too dang hard. At this point in the Mary Tudor, I have about eight inches completed but haven't picked it up in a couple of weeks. It's not that I don't want to work on her. Really. It's just that it's ninety-four degrees and we have no air conditioning. The idea of sitting around with a pile of wool in my lap is not very appealing at all.

One of Susette's current passions—the other is letterpress printing—is building a knitted abecedarium. Don't worry, I didn't know what it was either and had to ask.

Think of an abecedarium as a picture book of letters, where each letter has an object that represents it included in the design. For example, the illustration of *A* would have an *a* object in it, like an apple or an aardvark. Susette's abecedarium uses Fair Isle techniques to work up a majority of the motifs.

Her *A* is an artichoke. *J* is for jacquard. *N* is for Nantucket, the island, not the limerick. *K* is for Kelmscott, which was one of designer William Morris's houses in Oxfordshire. Each letter is documented on her blog in posts that walk the reader through Susette's creative process. Each is like a mini-lesson about, for example, Turkish rugs or Danish damask. Each comes with extensive footnotes and links full of nitpicky details that make a trivia hound's heart leap. Her blog is a catalog of exuberant obsessiveness.

The designs themselves are gorgeous, expertly mixing dark and light in a way that creates crisp details and a unified whole. They are even more breathtaking in person.

"My mother was not a knitter," Susette, who appears to be in her midforties and has a mass of dark curly hair, says when I asked her how she learned to knit. We're sitting in one of the many coffeehouses in Ithaca, where she obligingly agreed to meet me, a stranger, so that we could talk about Alice Starmore and Fair Isle knitting.

"She was not a knitter but did know *how* to knit. When I was maybe six or seven, I was fascinated with knitting and I wanted to know how to knit. She gave me some purple yarn and some needles and showed me how to do one or two things. It became a sort of huge, tangled mess. I had it for years.

"After that I just taught myself in little bits and pieces, especially when I was in college. There were lots of false starts but I was always really fascinated with it.

"I majored in art when I was in college, though my PhD is in art history. I still have a very strong creative urge. I'm very much drawn to the materials and the colors. So I like things that have interesting materials and interesting colors, but especially interesting colors. I like definition. I like really small things. In other words, I like process and technique more than the finished garment.

"It's always nice to finish things," she adds, smiling. "That's always a great sense of accomplishment. But it's also hard to let go of something. You always think, 'I could add a collar to that.' I love the process of knitting, especially Fair Isle. Other people say, 'How can you even embark on something like that that you may not finish for ten years or you may never finish?'"

Susette has had a couple of projects in her life for at least two decades, which proves how hard she finds it to let them go.

"The first colored sweater that I started on was a Kaffe [pronounced "Kayf"] Fassett," she says. Fassett is a Rowan designer who is known for using as many colors in one garment as he can get his hands on. "Why start small? I'm not timid about these things.

"I had no idea who he was. But I bought the yarn when I was in England and it was gorgeous, just gorgeous. I knew I couldn't get any more. At the time, twenty years ago, no supplier in this country was carrying that kind of yarn. I didn't know if any more was available even in England.

"My local yarn shop owner sold me the book of patterns for that yarn and she said, 'Okay. You can do this. It's just math.' So I did math and I followed Fassett's instructions, which were, basically, you're just going to knit with long strands.

"It was a disaster. The inside of it was like thrummed mittens. I got most of it done—and didn't have enough yarn to do it all. I cut it up and made pillows."

In spite of her difficulty finishing and letting go of projects, Susette has completed six Starmores. The first was a vest called Rosemarkie, which was named after a Pictish relic that was found in Scotland's Easter Ross area. The pattern is angular and features trapezoids overlying a horizontally striped background.

"Actually, Rosemarkie I've done twice, in two different colors," she says. "A friend of mine saw me making it and just fell in love with it. He was finishing his dissertation and I thought, 'Okay, I'll do two.' He wore it every day. I was glad it was appreciated.

"My own husband—I'd be happy to make him something but he doesn't like the look of Fair Isle. He likes solid colors. He wanted me to make him an argyle sweater and that just was not happening. I tried, but no. He's a big *Monty Python* fan. You know the Gumbys? With the Fair Isle vests? I like watching the Gumbys but I don't want to be one," she says.

Susette's abecedarium grew out of her letterpress and typography fixation. Due to an elbow injury, she'd stopped knitting anything larger than a child's sweater. Even those were worked on sporadically.

"Then during the fall a friend of mine told me about Ravelry. I joined just to see what was going on and it really inspired me. Really, really, really," Susette says.

"I had been so far out of the loop that I didn't realize how much blogging had become a real part of knitting," Susette says. "I was just blown away with what everyone else was doing and how everything was integrating so beautifully. So I thought, okay, I'll try something out, and it will have something to do with my interests, and those are knitting and letterpress printing and reading and history and art history."

Both Susette and I agree that the Internet has had a great impact on the way that knitters build communities. In the past, if you were lucky, you might have a yarn shop or a few knitters in your neighborhood. Now you can find thousands of them with just a few keystrokes. Most of them, fortunately, love to share what they've learned about the craft.

"There's so much more communication," Susette says. "When I started doing Fair Isle knitting, I was on a fellowship in Washington, DC. I was camping out at my parents' house. They happened to live within a mile of Yarns International, which is still going but it's not a retail store anymore. Now they mostly specialize in natural-colored Shetland.

"At the time they were a major supplier of Alice Starmore. She came through town and I got to take a workshop with her. This is when I was working on the first vest, so it has been touched by Her hand," Susette says, laughing. "*Herself* taught me to do Kitchener stitch."

Kitchener stitch is a method of grafting two rows of live stitches, which are the ones currently on the needles, together to make an invisible join. The bulk of knitters when forced to Kitchener will wind up setting the steps to a little jingle in their head. I asked Susette if she had heard the steps in a Scottish accent, since she learned from a Hebridean.

"Her accent is kind of interesting. It's not arch Scottish," Susette says, but she can't quite place what it does sound like.

"When I was with Yarns International, one of the first years that they got going, they actually would get knitters to knit Alice Starmores for them. That's how I got my Rona sweater. They gave me yarn and I knit them a sweater to be used for trade shows, then they gave it back to me. All I had to do was buy the buttons. It was great.

"I hung out [at Yarns, International] all the time. There was this nice little community there. That's when I first started sitting down with other knitters and looking at what they were doing and talking about what they were doing. I had been out of that for a long time until Ravelry. It's just amazing that you can find not only other people who are knitting but people who are interested in generally the same things you are interested in. I was amazed at how many knitters have typography habits. And there are quite a few letterpress printers too. It's really great to connect with them and find out what they're working on.

"Seeing what other people are doing really inspires me and gives me ideas. I've learned a lot, but it's more allowing my neurons to fire. I just really take it as a jumping-off point. It gave me permission, in a way."

Coincidentally, Susette just finished Donegal, the same Alice Starmore sweater that Ann Shayne is working on. Finishing a project like that will win you all sorts of accolades from knitters but may be met with suspicion by other people.

"When I finished it, I was so happy and so glad. All of my knitter friends were so supportive. I went into work and I told one of my friends at work that this was the sweater I just finished. In a staff meeting, she said, 'Oh, my God, I can't believe you made that.' Stunned silence followed.

"What I got out of that is that people thought it was unprofessional to have an obsession. It didn't seem as if they were recognizing it as a form of expression. It was like 'this is an obsession and obsession is not professional.' I actually felt uncomfortable after that."

Still, Susette knits—and documents what she has knit, both online and in physical form. She plans to bind the abecedarium swatches into a book. Fair Isle patterns keep calling to her too.

"I love the colors. I love the definition. I love that, in really traditional Fair Isle, it's a very logical pattern. I think most of all it's an assurance to me that there is this art that's not lost, that something of quality and of really high craftsmanship can still be made. I can do something that was valued and important and useful in the past—and valued and important now but maybe not so useful in quite the same way. Something that was made for everyday use before has now become a sort of art form," Susette says.

"Is that why you knit? To make an everyday object into a work of art?" I ask.

"I don't know why. I've always been fascinated with it. Part of it is the material. The color, the texture. Everything," Susette says.

"I used to do a lot of mixed media when I was studying art. The reason that I knit then was different from the reason that I knit now. Then it was—certainly I loved the feel, the texture and the look of it—but it was something about the tradition. It wasn't because it was a home-based handicraft. I had a sense of it as something that had been done for so long by so many people to produce something beautiful but useful.

"I can't say it was because it was something that my mother didn't do. It wasn't an act of rebellion. It is for some people. We're very close; my mother loves textiles. She was a docent at the textile museum in DC for many years. But the textiles that she gravitates to are rugs, because we lived in Turkey. Her interest in textiles had very much to do with our traveling.

"But for me—while I'm certainly interested in all of that too—it's different. I like the traditional aspects. She gave me her needles, which she still had," Susette says. "It's not that she's a really strong feminist, but she has very strong feminist ideas. I think for someone who was coming of age in the fifties, sixties, seventies, especially late sixties and seventies, knitting was just not something that fit in with her brand of feminism. But she supports me.

"And strangely enough, in his retirement years, my father suddenly took a shine to needlepoint. I have no idea why," Susette concludes.

My coffee with Susette is invigorating. Once I get home, I knit a dozen rows of Mary Tudor, growing ever more entranced with the pattern that I am making with my very own hands. My daughter, age six, is home from school and sitting at the other end of the couch flipping through an issue of *Ranger Rick*. Knitting with her brother both in the house and awake is impossible, since he is completely unable to not grab all the balls of yarn and toss them around the room like a dozen fibery footballs. But the girl and I can chill like this.

"Hey, Mom," she says, after an hour of relative peace. "That's pretty."

"Thanks." I say. "I like it too."

"When are you going to work on my hat?" she asks.

"What hat?"

"The one you said you'd make after I lost the last one you made. Out of the sparkly pink yarn? That one?"

Oh, I think. That hat. The one I forgot to start because Mary Tudor's siren pull was too great for a mere kid's hat.

"It slipped my mind, sweet pea. I'll get it to you by the winter."

She looks at me, shrugs, and goes back to her magazine.

5

June

To Quote Madonna: Get into the Groove

Audible.com subscription for $14.95 per month for 10 months: $149.50

After just a few short weeks of working on the body of Mary Tudor, I no longer have to focus every last drop of my attention on every last stitch. At first, just knitting for an hour left me feeling like a wrung sponge. I'd have to turn off the TV, chase away the kids, and corral the cats. The very act of making one stitch after another was all-consuming.

Three weeks in, two hours are no problem, brainwise. The TV can blare. The kids can run through the room with scissors. The cats can climb up my legs and back down again, driving little claw pitons into my calves as they go. I can knit through it.

I'm gobsmacked at how quickly my hands picked up the skill. It took me the better part of a semester to master a decent do-si-do when I took square dancing as a PE credit in college. Finding my groove on tiny little multicolored stitches only took a few weeks.

In fact, the work is growing tedious. Apart from having to know which color I need to make each stitch, the knitting itself is just that, knitting. No purls. No cables. No yarn-overs. Just knitting. Round and round and round again. With very small needles and very thin yarn.

Measurable progress is slow, simply because of how light the yarn itself is. I can knit for an afternoon and maybe have half an inch to show for it. I take great joy in rows 23–25 and 39–41 because I enjoy the way that Oasis, a sickly green, and Damson, a rich plum, play off each other. Other than that, the bigger problem right now is holding off the soul-crushing boredom.

I know. Something that appears to be so complicated ought to require more effort. Let this be today's life lesson.

Two things pull me through the work. The first is obvious: I want the sweater even more now that I know it's doable. The second is less so: I've discovered the wonders of the MP3 universe.

I knew about recorded books long before now. When I was getting to the gym on a regular basis, I used to check unabridged audiobooks out of the library all the time. To play on a portable cassette player, which should give you a sense of how long ago this was.

Since then, I've joined the twenty-first century (about four years after the rest of the world) and bought an iPod. I love it. That's not hyperbole. When it dies, I will mourn. I will also quickly buy another one before its little plastic body cools.

Without my iPod, so many chores would never get done. *This American Life* and *Radiolab*'s podcasts pulled me though last summer's complete scrubbing, wallpaper stripping, and repainting of my kitchen. *The Bugle* keeps me company on the walk to pick my daughter up at school or home from dropping her off. *Wait, Wait, Don't Tell Me*'s weekly podcasts give me the distraction I need to clean the house. Somehow, listening to these shows while also accomplishing something boring but necessary makes those hours feel virtuous.

Plus, the children have learned that it is best to not pester Mommy when she has the vacuum and her earbuds. No good ever comes of it.

There aren't enough podcasts to get me through all this knitting, however. I need something epic. Ann Shayne swears by Patrick O'Brian's boat books, which follow the ongoing adventures of two British Navy men during Lord Nelson's war. I nix these because I can't even think about seafood without feeling queasy. I briefly toy with listening to *Moby Dick* or *Atlas Shrugged*, simply because they are two books I ought to have read by now. *The Scarlet Letter* is another assigned book that I never finished and, shamefully, only read the Cliff's Notes for. Don't judge me. It's a really boring book, especially when you're fifteen and firmly believe that you already know everything.

What stops me from building my character with the classics is the reading I'm forced to do in my everyday life as a college instructor. There are days when it takes all the will

I have to read student essays or textbook chapters. Besides, the knitting itself is chore enough at this point. Why make it worse?

Instead, I give Audible.com a small amount of cash each month and give in to my guiltiest pleasures. One month it's Janet Evanovich's Stephanie Plum mysteries. The next month I wander Chicago with V. I. Warshawski. Then I fall down the Terry Pratchett's Discworld rabbit hole. My droll, charming best friend's voice visits me each time I pick up The Sweater and disappear into Ankh-Morpork.

(An aside: While the reviews on the Audible site bash narrator Celia Imrie and hyperpraise Nigel Planer, both are dead lovely. Besides, Imrie's voice reminds me of the wee British granny I never had. Her voice makes me feel like I've just had a perfect cup of tea and some buttery biscuits. Which is hard to evoke in someone whose childhood cultural memories largely revolve around pasta, red sauce, and guilt.)

To give you an idea of what the next six months look like from the outside, imagine me, with my gray-streaked hair and twenty extra pounds, sitting in a big green chair, tote bag of yarn next to me, iPod nearby, knitting.

What's going on inside, however, is more interesting. Susette's story about her mom starts me thinking about knitting (and other domestic pursuits) and feminism.

In a brief, highly unscientific poll—which means that I asked the women I know who are about the same age as I am—few of us can remember our moms knitting. A fair number of us, however, either can remember our grandmothers knitting or still have something that they made. Most of our moms are baby boomers; most of our grandmothers were raised during the Depression.

Enough folks came of age during the time when most women didn't knit to make those who currently do seem like throwbacks to a much earlier time. The last generation of women who knit in large numbers did so during the thirties and forties. Knitting was still enough of a cultural force that a popular poster during World War II featured a female hand with needles and yarn illustrating the slogan "Remember Pearl Harbor—Purl Harder."

It's hard to envision the same sentiment of "Let's knit warm things for our men over there" striking the same chord during the conflicts since. Yes, the wars (or police actions) during the last fifty years have been more politically fraught than WWII. The image of knitters has become fraught as well, if only because the image of women at work with yarn is stuck in our cultural imaginations as something that only happened "back then."

A comparison can be made between knitting and breast-feeding. Both skipped a generation when the wonders of the modern age were promoted over the methods of the past. When the traditional methods went mainstream again, they drew second glances when done in public.

During the decades between World War II and the first Gulf War, the chain of knitters was broken. There's an economic basis for this, certainly. Knitting machines and space-age yarns made store-bought sweaters cheaper than anything you could make at home. When you can buy a one-dollar pair of socks, you no longer need to know how to make them.

But the gap's roots dig deeper than mere practicality. Knitting—and other happy-hands-at-home crafts like sewing and crochet—became symbols of the domestic bubble that women were popping during feminism's second wave.

As historian Tobi M. Voigt put it in her thesis "Unraveling Myths: Knitting and the Impact of Feminism During the 1960s and 1970s," "Knitting and other domestic activities became entangled in the feminists' war against traditional sex-roles. Instead of viewing [handicrafts] as a vehicle for creative self-expression, many feminists saw these home-based and often family-focused activities as a manifestation of domestic obligations." In other words, along with their bras, women burned their mops, their cookbooks, and their yarn because they had become symbols of the patriarchy.

But that explanation is too facile. Plenty of women learned to knit during those decades. And not every woman in the civil rights/Vietnam era felt the feminist movement had a place in her life. Voigt, in fact, found plenty of women who admitted to needle use during that time, and she surveyed over 250 of them.

"American women who were active knitters during the 1960s and 1970s held a wide array of feelings and opinions about the feminist movement. Not unexpectedly, many of the women who continued to knit did not identify strongly with the feminist movement. They were happy as mothers and homemakers, and were largely unaffected by feminist suggestions that their hobby trapped them in the home.

"Regardless of their feelings about the feminist movement, 77 percent of the surveyed knitters asserted that feminism had no impact on their decision to knit. Unlike many feminists, the knitters did not perceive their hobby as a symbol of socially constructed gender roles. Instead, like Debbie from Kentucky, they repeatedly asked, 'What would feminism have to do with knitting?'"

What may have had a bigger effect on the number of knitters was the fallout from the feminist movement. Divorce became more acceptable, which meant that more women found themselves—either by choice or necessity—in the workplace. Also, the economic conditions of the Carter years forced greater numbers of women out of the house and into the office. More than anything else, this dramatic decrease in a woman's free time probably reduced the practice of knitting, especially now that it had become a creative pursuit rather than a pragmatic one.

To give an extremely localized example, my mom worked nine hours a day after she and my dad divorced, and also had to deal with all the required domestic chores like cooking, cleaning, and checkbook balancing. Every now and again, she'd have a minute or two to read, usually a Danielle Steele novel. As I got older and was better able to fend for myself, she invested some time in crochet, but even that was infrequent.

That's also true for the women in my unscientific survey. Most of my peers had moms who worked outside their homes during their childhoods, some because they took great pleasure in their careers, others because of financial necessity. Having a job and kids puts one heck of a crimp in what you can do during your off-hours.

My mother-in-law did manage to find time to knit, despite a divorce and a job. The projects, however, were job-related, since she knitted uteruses (uteri?) that she used during her childbirth education classes to demonstrate how the muscles contracted to push out a baby. Family lore has it that there are still some fiber wombs lurking in her basement.

By the 1980s, the yarn industry started to get hip to the reasons women weren't knitting as passionately as their forebears. According to Anne L. Macdonald, in her book *No Idle Hands: The Social History of American Knitting*, retailers too were realizing that " 'modern' women must cram knitting into already loaded schedules. Sensing this, Wild and Wooly Needlecrafts, a chain of shops in the Washington, DC, metropolitan area, targeted its press and radio campaign to a stereotypical customer, the career-oriented 'Wild and Wooly Woman' whose knitting competes for time with such contemporary activities as windsurfing, scuba diving, karate and skydiving." Which proves two things. First, the Wild and Wooly Woman might be an adrenaline junkie, and second, any social upheaval can be forged into a marketing tool.

Until recently, knitting struggled to find purchase in the minds of many women, who saw it as something grandmothers do while they rock in front of the fire. Turning the perfect sock heel was not what a modern career woman should spend her precious free time on, if only because she now had her own money to buy her socks and, if she wanted, throw them out after they developed holes.

Only in the last decade has knitting been able to shake the fusty old lady image, thanks largely to my generation of women and those much younger who discovered the craft—not because their moms knit, but because their friends do. The Internet makes connecting with other knitters so easy that the generational disconnect becomes a nonissue.

Yes, there are men who knit. But the stigma that surrounds men who knit has a different character from the one around women who knit. The assumption made about knitting men is that they are weak and girly and, in all likelihood, gay, not that there's anything wrong with that. Which is something you really want to bring up to a guy with needles in his hands who is sick to death of defending his choice of hobby. Regardless, that image (as well as the existence of lactating men, who may or may not knit) is outside the scope of this argument.

According to numbers crunched by Pearl-McPhee in *Free-Range Knitter*, there are 30 million golfers in the United States and Canada, with *golfer* defined as anyone who golfs to any degree. Compare that to 50 million knitters in the same region, with *knitter* defined as anyone who knows how to knit. The knitting industry brought in $8.5 billion in 2002, according to the Hobby Industry Association. Golf, according to a study by Golf 20/20, generated $38.8 billion, which is an order of magnitude greater, yes. But the golf start-up costs are greater to begin with. A cheap set of clubs will pull at least $100 out of your wallet; a cheap set of needles will cost $30.

Yet golf has invaded the cultural zeitgeist. There are cable channels and radio shows devoted to chasing a little white ball around so that you can knock it away from you again. A garage filled with clubs, balls, and Drizzle Stiks doesn't earn a second glance. Devoting an entire vacation to playing golf strikes no one as odd. Try doing the same with sheep and yarn.

My husband, a golfer, has dreamed of going to Scotland simply to visit St. Andrews, a links course that has frequently been the home of the British Open. No one ever asks him why he would want to do such a thing. When I mention that I'd love to go to Fair Isle just to visit the sheep, nonknitters look at me like I need a visit from the men with the huggy coats.

In short, if a man spends his free time pursuing a manly hobby, like chipping golf balls in the backyard, his time has been well spent. If a woman spends the same amount of time working on, say, a Fair Isle sweater named after the sister of Henry VIII, then she's just weird.

Stephanie Pearl-McPhee sums it up nicely. " 'It's about respect,' I told [her husband] Joe, and I meant it. Nobody tells golfers they are wasting their time. Nobody tells fishermen you can buy fish at the store and asks why anyone would bother to do it. At the end of the day, all debates exhausted, the only difference that I could divine seemed to be that golf was done mostly by men and knitting mostly by women, and that made one valid and the other vacuous."

Underneath the respect issue lurks another quagmire about ownership and tradition. For generations, knitting patterns were handed down. The hands of your grandmother taught the hands of your mother, which taught your hands. There were no authors.

The technical aspects were open-source as well. The knitters around you would show you the general process for constructing, say, a mitten. They'd also show you some basic ways to sex it up, to keep either boredom at bay or your creative mind engaged. Or, realistically, both.

Ownership of these pattern scaffolds wasn't really an issue. They were common knowledge that grew out of the connections among the crafters. Besides, there wasn't much point to ownership of something that had no discernible value. There was no knitting pattern market. You couldn't put a price tag on your knowledge about the knitting process, only the finished mitten.

Once geographical areas became known for certain types of garments, like Fair Isle for its warm, colorful sweaters, the fog of ownership became murkier. Those knitters' patterns began to have value—a distinctive look that it was in the knitters' best interests to protect. But how do you figure out who owns something that has been developed by many hands over time? Do you protect each motif? An entire garment's worth of motifs in that specific combination?

When the chain of knitters broke during the baby boom, these issues became a concern. My mother's hands didn't teach mine to knit. The patterns I use aren't my birthright. And selling new patterns to those like me can generate a lot of money for those who can catch my eye.

This puzzle of which parts of the process are protected also haunts the cookbook industry. You can't copyright the act of sautéing, but you can claim ownership of the specific written directions for what order you put your ingredients in a pan. Likewise, a designer can't claim the process of two-handed Fair Isle knitting, but she can put her mark on what order the colors go in.

This cookbook-based solution to knitting, however, raises as many questions as it answers. When the sweater is finished, who owns it? It's not like an entrée, which is consumed; a sweater lasts longer than a single meal. The designer can't demand a permissions fee from me every time I wear the sweater I made from her design, just as the cookbook author can't demand a royalty every time I make a dish from her book. But I can't reprint the recipe without properly attributing it to her and paying a royalty.

The questions get murkier. Can I take a picture of myself wearing the sweater I knitted and send it to a friend who may be able to work out the design and copy it? And if I make any changes to the design as written, who owns it now? If I make Rachael Ray's lasagna recipe but use sausage rather than ground meat, is it still her recipe? The answer is straightforward for the lasagna: if that's the only thing I change, I have to credit Rachael Ray and say that the recipe has been "adapted from" her book. But what if I use Cobalt yarn instead of Starmore's Delph?

Dr. Deborah Halbert in her essay "Feminist Interpretations of Intellectual Property," published in the always scintillating *American University Journal of Gender, Social Policy and Law*, unpacks the arguments about the current intersection of "women's work" like knitting and quilting with the legal construction of copyright. It's a crossroads for which we don't yet have an accurate map.

"After all, the pattern is only part of the creative process," Halbert writes. "The individual who does the knitting makes changes to the design, picks the colors of the yarn, and invests her unique motivation into the knitting process. The creative act of knitting transcends the pattern; yet, as copyright invades and colonizes this space, its users attempt to appropriate for themselves the claim to original creativity and seek to control the activity well beyond the construction of a pattern."

Starmore herself sneaks into Halbert's thoughts in footnote 58. "Ironically, Starmore's designs are all premised on the rich cultural heritage of her Scottish lineage and traditional Celtic designs; however, using the language of individual authorship and originality, she quickly ignores the traditions on which she draws in favor of a language of private property based on the exclusion of others," Halbert writes.

In short, despite complaints by her (or those who are protecting her marks) about copyright infringement, Starmore herself is mining cultural traditions in order to make her nut. While her spin on the components of any given design might be her creation, the architecture of it is not.

It's a dense knot to untangle, this whole issue of ownership. It gets pulled even tighter in a video Starmore made in 1994 for Butterick called *Fair Isle Without Fear*.

For a mere $275 on the used videotape market, you too can get your own copy of *Fear*. Or you can do what I did, which is drop into your local university library and request it through interlibrary loan. Then, if you are a lawbreaker, which I will neither confirm nor deny that I am, you could copy this tape onto a DVD. I do not endorse this course of action because that would be wrong.

I do recommend that if you have any interest in attacking a Fair Isle item, you should watch Starmore's explanation and demonstration of the technique. You will not find another that is more cogent and straightforward.

There are other reasons to watch it too. The video, which was recorded on Fair Isle during a photo shoot for a book of traditional knitting patterns, opens with shots of Shetland sheep, crashing waves, and puffins. A fiddle reel provides the soundtrack. For sheer escapism, the opening montage evokes a mini-getaway to a romantic land that is well worth the price of your library card.

Starmore herself walks you through the process of the technique of two-handed knitting and through the process of getting the wool. She has a friendly visit with Peter Jamieson of Jamieson's yarns, which is jarring given the rancor that seems to exist between them now. She talks to a shepherd, who kindly demonstrates how perfect his wool is for spinning very fine yarns. She shows swatches of traditional patterns and explains that the women of Shetland developed these motifs over decades of work.

But what raises my eyebrows is a segment near the end when she discusses color. Starmore suggests that if a given colorway isn't to your taste, then you should use the shades of nature to make it your own. Using colored pencils and a photocopy of a chart, she demonstrates how you can color in the squares until you come across a design that is pleasing to you.

Which is just a kick in the head, really. Here is one of the staunchest defenders of the sanctity of her knitting patterns showing you how to change them. If you can do that, then what is the copyright for? And if I wanted to knit her original design in hot pink and chartreuse and sell it as my own pattern, can I do that?

I find this all very confusing. Yet by watching this video, I clarify my feelings for Starmore herself.

As mean-spirited as it makes me sound, I want to dislike her. All the legal shenanigans about her brand leave a bad taste in my mouth. Even though I understand wanting to make money off your designs and yarn, I firmly believe that there has to be a less tone-deaf way to do it. Trying to achieve total control over every last iteration of your name leaves a trail of hard feelings. Yes, if you let some uses of it slide, you might miss out on a buck or two, but you will make up for it by not trashing your image.

In the days before networks of knitters were connected via the Internet, slighting a customer, as when one of your representatives tells a patron that she needs to get a life because her sniping is getting tiresome, wouldn't have global implications. But word spreads quickly now. Just ask Eliot Spitzer how long it took after his visit to the Mayflower Hotel before the bulk of his constituents knew about his affair. For knitters, gossip about a designer moves just as quickly.

My perception of Starmore as a hard-nosed businesswoman is shattered by the video. First, she's tiny. Wee enough to fold up and put in my pocket, which flies in the face of my mental picture of her as an imposing, windswept, ruddy-cheeked matron. Instead, Starmore has delicate features, almost translucent blue eyes, and dark hair in a pixie cut. And she looks uncomfortable on film. Like Martha Stewart during the first few seasons of her show, Starmore overenunciates every consonant in every word. You can see glimpses of panic in her eyes when she's not sure what to say next. Her hands shake as she holds up swatches. Her anxiety humanizes her enough that I drop my preconceived notions about who she is.

She seems most comfortable when talking about the inspirations for her designs, how she uses her swatches as postcards. The shapes and colors serve as visual reminders of a place or a time. This swatch is about a hike in the Scottish Highlands—and darned if it doesn't look exactly like a walk in the woods should look. Another swatch captures an especially brilliant sunset on the Isle of Lewis, which she almost doesn't need to explain because that is so clearly what those colors represent.

During this bit of show and tell, Starmore's mastery of the craft is obvious. Also obvious is how important it is to use the yarns she has specified in the colors also specified. Her hard-assed approach leads to the best result.

My non-hard-assed approach—where I use a different brand of yarn altogether and completely ignore one of the colors—makes me wonder if the Alice Starmore sweater that I'm knitting will actually be an Alice Starmore when the last bit is knitted.

6

July and August

Knots in the Skein

Video entitled *Fair Isle Without Fear*, hosted by Alice Starmore: $275 (or free with library card)

Before I get too wrapped up in my existential dilemma about what makes an Alice Starmore an Alice Starmore, life intervenes and I have to fly to Pittsburgh, my hometown.

My grandfather's death isn't a huge surprise. When you hit ninety, it's pretty clear that your personal alarm clock is close to ringing. He remained in decent health for nearly all those ninety years, which was a blessing.

While it isn't a sudden shock, it is still very sad. He was a decent, wonderful man whose loss leaves a void in the lives that his touched. The depth of my own grief surprises me. It sneaks up on little cat feet and bites me during the church service.

I haven't been in a church—much less a Catholic one—in years. You never really forget the emotions that religion has a knack for evoking. Guilt has always been one of them, for me, anyway. But few other institutions are as good at channeling hope and grief.

I cry through most of the Mass, which is so unexpected that I don't even have a tissue. My dad gives me the soft, white handkerchief that he always has with him, something that he hasn't done since I was a kid. The memory of all the times one of those handkerchiefs wiped my nose or dried my tears makes me cry even more, because I know that sooner than I'd like to imagine, my dad won't be there to hand me a handkerchief when I need one.

During the drive from the church to the cemetery, which takes about thirty times longer than anticipated because the parkway is never swift, I want more than anything to knit a round or two of Mary Tudor, which is almost knitted to the armholes. But the sweater is now big enough that it is too cumbersome to fly with. I've taken to carrying all the little balls of yarn with me so that I won't have to stop to hunt for them. The sweater's tote bag grows more awkward each week. I'm certain that it won't fit in an overhead bin, provided the TSA would let me on a flight with it in the first place. The idea of checking it fills me with dread. What if it got lost? I need to lie down even now when I think about it.

I went with my better judgment and left Mary T. at home. But the knitting has gone from cursed to comforting. That unwieldy tote bag of yarn is my very own woobie or blankie. And I wanted my woobie right now, in the same way that my oldest child needs her blankie when life knocks her around.

My grandfather was a Navy man during World War II.

In honor of his service, two seamen at the cemetery drape his coffin in the American flag, which they then fold and present to my aunt. When the younger of the two thanks her for her father's service, his sincerity is palpable. We all dissolve into tears. Even my father, a man I can remember crying only once previously, dabs at his eyes with yet another clean, white handkerchief.

"Knit on with confidence and hope through all crises," Elizabeth Zimmerman preached. That's just what I want to do. The knitting itself, sadly, is hundreds of miles away.

The act of knitting provides comfort in times when life weighs the most. Even great women found that their needles and their yarn provided succor.

Marie Antoinette "was thwarted as well when she asked to be given the needlework she had begun in the Temple; once again, she expressed her eagerness to finish making a pair of stockings for her son. Although Madame Elisabeth and Madame Royale packed up the materials and sent them to the Conciergerie, the officers refused to give them to the Queen, on the grounds that she might hurt herself with the needles. Desperate for something to do in her barren cell, and perhaps anxious to provide her son with clothing of a nonrepublican provenance, Marie Antoinette resorted to picking threads out of the faded, torn tapestry that hung on the wall over her bed. Using a pair of toothpicks, she 'knitted' these threads into a pair of garters which she begged the prison concierge to send to the Temple. The gift never reached Louis Charles, who died under mysterious circumstances in prison," wrote Caroline Weber in *Queen of Fashion: What Marie Antoinette*

Wore to the Revolution. Think what you will about the circumstances that put her in the Conciergerie, but you must agree that keeping her from her work in progress was cruel.

I don't have to resort to toothpicks and threads picked from the funeral home's wall-to-wall carpet, however. Trish, one of my former college roommates and current best friends, lives in the 'burgh. She is the kind of friend you can call to let know you'll need her guest bed in less than twenty-four hours during the middle of the workweek. She's also the kind of friend who won't go crazy cleaning up before you get there, because you're like family.

We've known each other for more than twenty years. And while it's been almost that long since we've lived in the same city, we've still kept in touch through poor decisions and smart ones, in sickness and health, during weddings and births.

Until recently, Trish was a cross-stitcher, which cut down on the amount of craft-related bonding we could do. In the last few years, she's taken up knitting, which makes my heart do a little caper of joy. Because she's a knitter, she knew the best balm for my grief. We go to a yarn shop.

(Actually, we first go to the Trader Joe's across the street, because the other recommended balm for tender feelings is TJ's peanut butter cups. After a few of those are medicinally applied, we go to the yarn shop.)

Yarn shops, like people and dogs, have their own distinct personalities. I have been in establishments that, despite selling a fiber spun to keep you warm, were so cold that I left with frostbitten fingers. Some are comfortable. Some, like Purl in

New York City, is so tiny that you have to step outside to pull out your wallet, which I do a lot at Purl because their stock is expertly curated.

My own local yarn shop shares a space with a gourmet food/spice shop. All your purchases smell of exotic, indefinable lands. The shop is inviting, if just for the smell. Nancy, its proprietor, is welcoming as well. My knee-jerk response is to want to tidy the stock, but that is a reflection of my own compulsiveness.

Natural Stitches, located in a strip mall in Pittsburgh's Eastside, overcomes its beige location by brimming with both yarns and geek pride. These are the knitters who have strong feelings about an afterthought sock heel versus a slip-stitch sock heel, even though both work just fine, and have no qualms about debating the topic for hours, not because their way is the right way but because debating is fun.

By comparison, Knit One, another shop not far from Natural Stitches in tony Squirrel Hill, feels like a place to hang out after your Pilates class. It has its own charms, especially on the days when long discussions about the merits of a cable cast-on hold no appeal. For me, Knit One is an escape to another life, whereas Natural Stitches is closer to where I already live.

On an evening when I've spent the last few hours tangled in my own unexpected grief, nothing could provide more comfort than a wall full of all the Cascade 220 glorious colors. I fondle the luxury yarns, the silks and cashmeres that I can never afford. I cuddle some gorgeous hand-dyed sock yarn and find myself falling in love. Linen yarn in the exact two shades of my bathroom wink at me from a shelf, and I buy them to make a hand towel.

Trish and I leave, bags in hand, made whole enough again to weather life's next storm.

Knitting as solace against life's upheavals is not a new idea. But is knitting "the new yoga," as it was dubbed by Lily Chin in 2002? Having done both with some regularity, I can attest that I have never broken a good sweat while knitting, nor have I ever left my yoga practice with a new scarf. Knitting is knitting, oddly enough. And yoga is yoga. Which is pretty Zen when you think about it. Nevertheless, I pack my bag to talk to Cyndi Lee, an internationally acclaimed yoga instructor and the founder of New York City's Om Yoga studio. Cyndi is also a knitter.

"I've been very ambitious my whole life," she says. "I don't even realize it. I just keep going. My husband says, 'You keep picking door number three. You say you're tired and you don't want to do anything, but you keep picking door number three.'

"But in knitting, I don't have that ambition because it's really about the doing. At this point in my personal yoga practice, I also feel that way. I love to do yoga and I do it every day, but I don't have the feeling like I once did when I was younger that I really want to do that super-fancy pose. Now it's just more about being connected.

"[Yoga guru] Mr. Iyengar's favorite definition of yoga is also my favorite, which is integration. You're pulled in a million directions, and when you do yoga, it's a gathering together, a gathering of energy. And that's what happens with knitting.

"That's one of the things that's really hard for people in meditation. So many people think right away, 'I want to meditate.' The first day we offer meditation class, we get like fifty people there. The second day, there's like two.

"It's so hard to sit still. You find out that there is a technique and there's sort of something to do but not anything to do with your body, and it feels like you're not doing anything. In knitting, you get to do something. Your mind is pretty focused, at least at my level of knitting. I have to pay attention. I have to wear my glasses. I have to be on it to a certain degree. When I turn the heel [on a sock she's knitting], I have to turn off the TV and say, 'Don't talk to me.'"

"It was knitting that made me realize how hard it can be to count to ten," I say.

"That's so interesting," Cyndi responds, "because a Zen technique of meditation is counting the breaths. They say nobody ever gets to ten. Our mind strays. It's considered to be unbelievably advanced as a meditator if you can hold your mind for two breaths. Seriously. Counting to ten is really hard. So when you do it, you feel like, 'I did something.'"

Perhaps the best advertisement for the restorative powers of yoga is spending a few minutes in a room with Cyndi. She is infectiously warm and bubbly. Despite being in her midfifties, she has the energy of a much younger woman. Not that fifty is old by any means, but when she tells me her age, I'm completely stunned.

I'm trying to figure out what it is that I am knitting when

I am knitting Mary Tudor. Have my small substitutions taken me far enough off the true path that I'm now working on something very similar to but not a Starmore? Who better to ask than a yogini and knitter?

Cyndi, like so many of us knitters, learned to knit first as a kid. It didn't stick. Sewing became her main love throughout high school and well into adulthood.

"I had this overwhelming urge to quilt about ten years ago," she remembers. "I Googled 'quilting,' because I didn't know what else to do. Somehow, Downtown Yarns came up, which was two blocks from my house. I went over there and started drooling over the yarn. I forgot even the word *quilting*. The store was closing and the owner said, 'You have to leave. But I can give you a lesson tomorrow at the bagel store across the street.' And that was that.

"I took a couple of lessons from her. It came back immediately. Then I got hooked on it. I teach yoga all over the world, so I am in hotel rooms and airports by myself a lot. And I'm on airplanes, flying to India, flying to Hong Kong. There's nothing better to do than knit. That just got me hooked.

"Finally, one of my yoga friends taught me how to knit socks. I went to her house—I was teaching a workshop in Ohio and I was staying in her house—and my suitcase was half-full with the blanket I was working on. She's like, 'Oh, come on. This is silly. Please let me teach you to make socks.' Now I've been making socks like a maniac and loving that.

"I really like making my own socks," Cyndi says. "I like having really short socks so I can make them exactly mine. That's the beauty of it. I found out that it's not as much fun to make socks for men. I made a pair of socks for my friend, Christopher Guest, who is my husband's best friend from childhood. He turned sixty this year and we flew out to their home in Idaho for a birthday weekend. I made socks for him. It took *for-ev-er*. I finished one sock, and the other one wasn't finished by the end of the weekend. I gave the finished one to him. Then I said, 'Give it back to me so I can finish the other one and I'll mail them to you.'

"I finally mailed them to him. He just sent me an email: 'Thank you so much for the socks. I love them. They're luscious. I especially like the right one.'"

The sock-knitting impulse is hard to explain to nonknitters. Why on earth would you spend so much time on an item that is so pedestrian? Why waste precious hours on a project that few people will ever see? More importantly, why make something that is destined to wear out quickly?

For me, the sock-knitting impulse is twofold. First, modern sock yarns, whether wool or cotton, are absolutely gorgeous. Indie dyers—folks like Sundara, whose limited edition hand-dyed yarns, some skeins of which cost upward of fifty dollars, are snapped up as soon as they go on sale on her site—tend to start with sock-weight yarns.

Secondly, socks are portable. Once you get the basic recipe down, you don't need to look at a pattern. I take my socks in progress with me whenever I fear I'll have to wait for more than a few minutes. I almost never intentionally sit down to knit on a sock. Instead, each sock I've made owes its existence to all those weird little minutes of idleness at the dentist, say, or watching a student talent show.

Yes, socks, even hand-knitted ones, get holes. The only way to avoid loving your socks to death is not to wear them, which seems to deny them the opportunity to fulfill their destiny. So what if they wear out? If you're deeply disturbed by the ephemeral nature of all things, you could darn them. But sensible knitters darn differently, by holding the holey sock over the trash, muttering "Darn it," and letting go. Rather than a crisis, this is just an opportunity to knit more socks.

For some sock knitters, there's a third reason, which Cyndi mentioned. Like all knitwear, socks can be customized to fit your particular feet. This isn't as much of a selling point for me, if only because I've never been that dissatisfied with my store-bought sock options.

While Cyndi has no fear of socks, there are some projects that daunt her. "Basically anything that has to fit. That's partly because I hate my body, which is another subject. I used to be a professional dancer, and you get obsessed. It's a neurosis. I'm afraid I'm going to make a sweater and it's going to be too tight and I'm going to feel bad. It just seems impossible to make something that actually fits," she says.

"That's what I like about Mary Tudor," I explain. "The pattern is for just one size. That's it."

"But is that going to look good?"

"Probably not. But it's about finishing it, not wearing it," I say.

"I get that. This is one of the similarities to yoga. The joy is in the journey, to be totally clichéd about it. It's in the doing. The thing that's even cooler about yoga—not that you could even say that—is that yoga is called a practice. Internally and physically, it's a practice for later. The strength is going to show up when your baby runs down the street or you need to move your furniture or carry your groceries. Your stamina will show up. Your stability will show up," she explains.

"But it's not a rehearsal, in another sense. You're doing it now. Knitting is the same way but you get something at the end. I don't have such a feeling about wanting to make something for myself. The making of the thing itself is just a delight.

"I did a knitting and yoga retreat a couple of years ago and I've been threatening to do another one. It was really interesting because it was definitely easier to have a lot of different levels of knitters on that retreat, rather than different levels of yogis. We had some young women who were already hard-core yoginis and wanted a strong practice. Then there were a lot of women who were older than me who had never done yoga and were thinking, 'Now's the time.'

"The good news is that most advanced yogis don't mind going slower. If you have a good-enough teacher leading you, then he or she can work with an advanced person in a deeper way, even while going a lot slower. Plus I brought an assistant who is also a really good knitter. That was perfect and fun for her. We were able sometimes to go a little faster and she could stay with the slower people and help them. Between the two of us, we were able to take care of it.

"Then when you're knitting, you sit in a circle and everybody helps each other and it works out. There were some people who had never knit before and were learning. And there was one guy who was a real master knitter and a very good yogi who was making something with cashmere." I can see Cyndi almost sigh when she mentions the cashmere.

"It was really fun," she says. "I would know how to do it better now."

My yoga résumé is much shorter than my knitting one, even though I've been practicing both for about the same length of time. I learned from a hard-core Iyengar teacher in Knoxville, which is a jargon-rich way of saying that his instruction was all about form. Ron Felix's step-by-step directions for, say, Warrior I, a standing pose where you extend your arms and lower your trunk, included precise measurements of degrees, as in, your left foot is at ninety and your right foot is at sixty-five. At times he would specify which groups of muscles should be lifting and rotating which way and for how long.

Ron's biomechanical framework was perfect for me because the New Agey blue smoke and woo-woo and crystal approach to anything—especially a form of exercise—has always put me off. It was the introduction to yoga the skeptic in me needed.

Just as I learned enough about the basics of a few forms to pass muster with Ron and graduate to level 2, which took longer than you might imagine, my husband and I moved to Oneonta. Yoga classes are few and far between up here. The closest big city is an hour away and we are too far from Woodstock and the other Catskill towns to benefit from their trendier pull. Eventually I lucked into another teacher, who introduced me to Vinyasa yoga.

If Iyengar is about form, Vinyasa is about flow. It's here I learned how one pose can connect to the next and, more important, why you might want it to. I learned how to breathe. And I learned how to laugh. I had laughed before, but I think flow yoga taught me how moving my body can give me the giggles.

I started to see the glimmers of all the other aspects of yoga, the woo-woo parts that I'd dismissed before. Then I had a second baby and wandered onto a new path, one where a nap was much more fulfilling than a Downward Dog. By the time I was ready to get back to my practice, that teacher had sold his studio and left on an extended spirit quest of sorts.

For a variety of reasons, most having to do with my own laziness, I haven't found a new teacher. If the three-hour one-way commute weren't an obstacle, I'd haunt Cyndi's Om Yoga studio like a benevolent ghost who can't resist a good Sun Salutation.

To jump back a few ideas, most knitting is more a Vinyasa or flow state than an Iyengar pursuit. It is about what the craft feels like for you, not about getting the technique absolutely correct.

"One of the things I really like when I was relearning to knit," Cyndi says, "was it seemed like everybody gave me the same message, which is, if it works for you, you're doing it right. If you're a loose knitter, that's interesting. If you're a tight knitter, that's interesting.

"I turned out to be a loose knitter. So this pattern is for size two needles and I use zeros and that's interesting. I secretly think that it's kind of cool to be a loose knitter, but it can also be interesting to be a tight knitter. That's something that I really think is great about knitting that as a yoga teacher has gone into my teaching. It's helped me to articulate. I say that to people all the time in class.

"Yoga's not task-oriented," Cyndi says. "It's not a project mentality. It's long-term. Whatever you notice, you take the meditation approach of, 'Oh. That's interesting.' You just observe it. You don't even let it go.

"For example, I want to make a sock. I go to Purl. Leah, who comes to yoga here and works at Purl, says, 'This would be a good one for you to start with.' She gets me set up. I go home. I make it. I put it on. And it's huge. I go back and I say, 'Leah, look at my sock.'

"She says, 'You're really a loose knitter. Let me measure.' She measures it. She does her little calculations, which are all beyond me. She says, 'You need size zero needles. Go home with these now and make your sock.' I go home and the sock fits.

"It's not even just letting go, because then you'd say, 'Oh, well, they're too big. Whatever.' No, you look at it. You sit with it. And through that you find a solution to working with that obstacle."

"And," I add, "to working with who you are."

"Right. The idea of an obstacle actually shifts to 'This is the situation at hand.' That's been an interesting way to teach. Like, 'Oh, your arms are too long? Your arms are too short? You're tired? That's interesting. Whatever you are feeling is interesting. Don't throw that away.' Keep that on the mat with you and explore that in relationship to this particular pose right now as it is. And the practice opens up.

"If I'm scared of making something, it's because I want

a teacher because it's just a little bit overwhelming to try on my own. But it's not a fear of really doing it wrong. Knitting feels very open and spacious. That has been my experience in every knitting situation I have been in."

When Cyndi says that, I realize how knitting (and yoga, to a lesser extent) has changed me. My standard response to obstacles is to ignore them, no matter how enormous they may be. I don't work around them, mind, or climb over them. Put a boulder in front of me and I will stand with my face pressed against it until the sheer force of my will makes it shift.

This works about as often as you'd think. When I first started to practice yoga, I would force my fingertips to my toes, even though my body fought against that. Like raising my children, writing a book, or teaching a class, I wanted to do yoga right. I wanted the praise for my ability to be perfect, no matter how much my pursuit of this mythical perfect state hurt me.

I wish I'd found yoga sooner, but I don't know that I would have been ready to learn this lesson before I had kids and before I learned how to knit. Those had to come first. So many child-related obstacles, from potty training to back talk, can't be overcome through sheer force of parental will. If they could, my oldest child would have been using the toilet at fourteen months and would follow my every command.

I'm laughing just thinking about that. She's gotten the shoving-against-any-obstacle gene too. There's no reward in this zero-sum game. One of us has to be able to say, "That's interesting," and open the practice up. I'm the grown-up; it has to be me.

Knitting is good practice for that. If the sleeve isn't working out, pushing against it won't change it. I can stop. I can breathe into the pause. And I can decide to take a step to the left. I can also decide to call it a few names before I meet the problem where it is. My enlightenment goes only so far.

"When does a Starmore cease being a Starmore?" I ask Cyndi, since the yoga-inspired answer may be the one I need. "With one of her patterns, you don't mess with it. What happens if I do?"

"How would she know?" Cyndi responds. "If I thought of it in yoga terms—you told me you learned Iyengar yoga. If you learn Iyengar yoga, you can do any other style of yoga. You have a great foundation. You have learned the alignment principles. You have learned the basic philosophy principle of yoga, which is connection and union of apparent opposites. You press down to lift up. As Mr. Iyengar said in an intensive I got to take with him, 'I spent my whole life studying the effects of my action in the form of what happens to my sternum when I press my big toe down right now.' Something happens with every action that you make. So you cultivate a certain kind of awareness.

"What that means to me is, at a certain level, if you're doing yoga, even if you're using Iyengar methods, it's your yoga or it's no yoga. It has to be personal, or else it's not a practice. It's somebody else's practice and you're copying it. Until it integrates and becomes your personal experience, what is *my* toe doing right now, not what is Mr. Iyengar's toe doing, and how does that effect *my* sternum, right now, today, in this pose. Not what happened yesterday. What is happening right now. That's your yoga.

"That's the same as 'This is called knitting and this is called purling,' whoever you are. And you make loose ones but still that's a knit stitch and that's a purl stitch. It's yours. If you're making it, it's your sweater. Whether you use the same yarn as Alice Starmore, it's still your yarn. It's your doing. It's your expression of an Alice Starmore sweater.

"Let me ask you a question," Cyndi says. "When I just gave you my answer, how did that make you feel? Do you feel that you should respect and obey and always call it an Alice Starmore? Or yes, that is *my* sweater. I made it."

"I feel two ways about it," I say, because I do. "I can see the point that the sweater I am knitting is my sweater. However, when you start an Alice Starmore sweater, you know that it has to be the colors that Starmore had. If you're going to knit one of her patterns, you just do it. You have to surrender to her ideas."

"That's interesting too, that surrender idea," Cyndi says. "If you think of that in yoga or Buddism, it's the same thing. In a way, you won't be able to find that personal connection until you surrender to the teacher, a good, honest, healthy teacher. There's no sense in going to a class and he says, 'Turn your foot this way,' and you say, 'No. I don't believe in that.' And some people are like that. We all have resistance in different ways. Part of the practice and part of the deepening is the teacher's voice. It is like water on the rock, softening the sharp edges. Then you get to the essence of the rock. That's when you do start to have your own practice."

"With some knitted items I feel that I am already the soft rock," I say. "But with this Fair Isle project, I'm letting her tell me what to do because I don't see it the way she sees it. I look at the colors heaped in a bag and think that she's nuts for putting them in the same sweater. Now that it's coming together, I have these moments where I'm like, 'Oh. That's interesting.'"

"That means you're already the soft rock because you're open. Have you heard that Buddist thing about the teacups? There's the teacup that has a little crack in it, so that when you pour tea in it, the tea just goes right out. And then there's the teacup that's already full, so you pour tea and it just overflows. Then there's the teacup that's turned over. The best teacup—or the best student—is the empty cup.

"We tell that story to our students on the very first day of teacher training. When they're ready to take teacher training, it means that they know something already. They've been studying yoga for a while. Some of them come in like a full cup. But it sounds like you're already an empty cup. For as much as you know and as much as you've experienced, you know that you need to empty your cup to be able to make this thing that this person on her island has figured out for you. But your experience is still going to be your experience making it."

Since I am in New York City to talk to Cyndi, I decide to take my sweater out for visits with the folks I like to see when I make the trek in.

First stop is my editor's office, where I go just to prove that I am working on a tangible project. I fail to mention that I've not done a whole lot of actual writing yet. If you are holding this book in your hands, then my omission mattered little and it all worked out in the end.

I'm far enough along in the knitting—up past the beginnings of the armholes—that you can get a sense of Alice Starmore's genius. I don't rely on my reaction to it, if only because some of its magic has lessened for me, but the reactions of other people reinforce for me the brilliance of the sweater.

When I pull Mary Tudor out of its tote bag, people stop. Their eyes get big. One hand reaches out, then stops until I tell the person it's okay to touch it. Mary Tudor is mesmerizing.

What's also great is that most nonknitters think I'm a genius for figuring out how to knit it. I always explain that it's not as hard as you think. I explain that once you get the trick, it couldn't be easier. Yes, it's time-consuming, but it's not difficult. No one believes me, choosing instead to think that I am a master of hand-eye coordination. I'm okay with that.

My editor dubs the sweater Lana, after Lana Turner, who was called the Sweater Girl for wearing a form-fitting one in *Love Finds Andy Hardy*. *Lana*, conveniently, also means "wool" in Spanish. Afterward, Lana and I continue our schlep across the city.

We stop to see Ellen Kushner, who is the host of NPR's *Sound and Spirit*. She's also a great speculative fiction writer, which is how I know her. I pull the sweater out of my bag and she gets the same dreamy look in her eyes that everyone at my editor's office had. "It looks like a tapestry," she says. Then we take Lana out for Thai food and gossip. Ultimately, Lana and I are destined for Kay Gardiner's apartment. Kay, the other half of Mason-Dixon Knitting, has agreed to put me up for a night and to talk about knitting.

"I learned as a kid," Kay says. We're back at her apartment after a trip to the Fairway, a grocery store in her neighborhood that should be in the guidebooks as a bona fide tourist attraction. We've just supped on a yummy salad niçoise and one of the better chocolate chip cookies I've had in, like, ever.

Kay has settled in with her Knitting Olympics project, which is a kid's sweater. The Knitting Olympics was dreamed up in 2006 by Stephanie Pearl-McPhee, the source of so many modern knitting group activities. Somehow, the Yarn Harlot has become the Julie McCoy of the knitting community's *Love Boat*. The goal is to find a project that will challenge your skills and that can be completed during the two-week span of the Olympic games. Knitters are encouraged to embrace the ideal of "Citius, Altius, Fortius" or "Swifter, Higher, Stronger." For the summer 2008 games, Ravelry groups (and others) carry the organizational torch, since Pearl-McPhee, a Canadian, will only handle organization duties for the winter games.

"I was in the Campfire Girls, who are now called Campfire USA because it's boys and girls. I was probably ten or eleven, fifth or sixth grade. My Campfire leader was this woman who smoked cigarettes and had a very mean dog. She was a good knitter. She taught us how to knit. I made one pair of little bootee slippers out of red acrylic—that sort of fire engine red, tomato red, fakey red acrylic yarn. They had pom-poms. I imagine that she must have done a lot of the knitting for me because I remember knitting a little bit, then all of a sudden I had slippers.

"My mom wasn't crafty at all. Her craft is cleaning," Kay says. "There just wasn't any continuation of it. I didn't have yarn or needles in the house. So I just forgot about it. But I did like it."

"Were Campfire Girls like Girl Scouts?" I ask. Kay grew up in the Midwest, which was more of a Campfire Girl stronghold than western Pennsylvania, where I grew up.

"Campfire Girls has a lot of craftiness in it," Kay explains. "The Girl Scouts had the badges. We had no badges. We had beads. So you earned beads, these beautiful wooden beads. Every year there'd be a ceremony where you'd get your beads, then you'd arrange them on this navy blue felt vest in patterns of your choosing. The really anal-retentive girls had them all lined up. I don't really remember how I first put them, but at one point I renovated my vest, snipped them all off, and I'm not sure I ever got them all back on. But I started putting them in like—this was the early seventies—daisies. I made a tapestry of my beads. I hope to find that someday."

As it does for so many knitters, time passed.

"Many years later I was living in New York," Kay says. "This was when I was a big runner. Before knitting, I did running, which was a healthier sport, although you won't wreck your hip or your knees knitting."

I almost mention knit-induced carpal tunnel but don't want to bring the conversation to a screeching halt so that we can chant mystical invocations to ward off the ailment, like medieval man did to keep the plague at bay. Hand pain is perhaps the biggest injury a knitter can acquire. Blindness may be second.

Shortly after she gave up running, Kay "was walking by a yarn store on Broadway. I ran the marathon in 'ninety-two, so I think it was 'ninety-two or 'ninety-three. I went upstairs to see what they had there.

"I asked them, 'I think I remember how to knit. Can I try and see if I do remember?' So somebody handed me some yarn that was already cast on onto needles and I remembered how. I had this sudden certain knowledge that I was going to buy some yarn and make something. Of course hindsight is always twenty-twenty, but I'm pretty sure that this is true, that standing in that store I knew that I was going to be a knitter. I was like, 'This is *awesome*.'

Kay spent the next decade in a knitter-free wilderness.

"Nobody in my life was knitting. I was a lawyer for ten years after that. It was just kind of a weekend thing and a winter thing, but I would get really into it. It helped that my husband wanted me to watch sports with him that I wasn't really interested in. I like some sports but this was March Madness, all of those college teams that you've never heard of. He would want me to sit there with him. This is pre-kids.

"Knitting gave me something to do, and I could be happy

watching the basketball game while I was knitting. I would put it aside from time to time. It wasn't at all obsessive but it was intense. I really liked it, in just the same way that I do today."

Kay, by her own admission, isn't daunted by mere knitting projects. Her approach to the craft is fearless. So far, it has worked for her.

"Maybe it's the Campfire Girl in me, but once I knit that first sweater, I would just go into a yarn store, look through the patterns. Whatever I thought was pretty and that I wanted to knit, I would just say, 'I'm knitting that.' I was always biting off more than I could chew."

I did the exact same thing when I learned to knit. Back in my hat phase, I'd pack the baby up and head to my local yarn shop when I needed more hat yarn. She'd sit on the shop's floor in her car seat, where the women who ran the place would entertain her while I'd get lost in all the yarn. The shop owner suggested that it was time to make a sweater, reasoning that if I could knit, purl, and bind off, a sweater was well within my grasp.

At the time, as I stood there gritty-eyed from sleep deprivation, that made total sense. I found a pattern for a boxy V-neck pullover. I bought some acrylic seafoam green worsted weight from the bargain bin. When I got home, I cast on.

My first sweater attempt, unlike Kay's, ended in an epic failure. The sweater's design would never flatter my chest-heavy apple body. The color looked awful on me, even when I was not spectrally pale from spending so much time indoors with a new baby. Worst of all, the pattern was too easy. Just mile after seemingly endless mile of stockinette stitch, with the relative excitement of a decrease stitch very thin on the ground.

I kept setting it aside to knit more hats, which are done just as they start to get boring. Five years later, after finishing the front, back, and one sleeve, I ripped it all out and recycled the yarn into the world's ugliest triangular shawl, which I wear only in the comfort of my own home. What it lacks in aesthetic appeal, it makes up for in warmth. But if I accidentally set it on fire while cooking, I won't cry.

Kay had better luck with her first projects.

"I knit this Debbie Bliss Norwegian baby sweater that had reindeer and snowflakes on it," she says. "It was Fair Isle, which I did not even know the word for. I understood logically that the chart meant that you figure out some way to switch colors but totally improvised. I didn't know any techniques for doing it. That baby is now twelve and her parents kept this sweater because it turned out beautifully.

"It was beginner's luck. I had no concept. I guess it was hard, but it was like a crossword puzzle or Sudoku: it wasn't unpleasant. In fact, I now don't do anything that's unpleasant. I'll just stop if there's something I don't like about the yarn or the technique. I don't particularly like intarsia. I've done it when I've really wanted the thing because it was really beautiful."

Readers of her blog know that Kay has a fondness for knitting big things, like sweaters for her late husband, who was six seven, or bed-sized blankets.

"I'm not intimidated at all by the size of something.

Frankly I don't understand people who are. You like to knit. What is the problem with knitting more? Is it that you want to achieve a certain count of knitted things? To me, it's all about 'Do I want to make this thing?' If I want to make this thing, it's a pleasure for me to do it. In the middle of a blanket, if I'm sick of it, I really find that if I put it aside for a while, it comes back to me."

Unlike her cohort Ann in Nashville, Kay doesn't have a big stash of yarn lurking in the garage. This might be a by-product of having lived for years in a New York City apartment with two kids and a very tall spouse. Or it could just be part of Kay's minimalist philosophy of knitting, which is that you should knit what you absolutely love right now.

"My husband thought that I have a huge yarn stash, but I have fifteen pairs of shoes and he thought I had a lot of shoes. I'd say, 'Honey. This is nothing. This is not "shoes." This is just something to cover my feet. If I had a lot of shoes, you'd be seeing some shoes around here.'

"With yarn, I want to have what I know I'm going to use. I have like the flour and sugar yarn, the stuff that I use for my blankets: denim and various brands of cotton in many, many colors. I don't feel deprived."

Kay is not a project snob. Knitters should feel free to take on projects that speak to them.

"I really think that you should knit what you want to knit, what is fun for you to knit. Which is why I don't understand people who are down on knitting dishrags. Do I think anyone needs a knitted dishrag? No. But I like to knit them."

"What is the appeal of making something like a dishrag,

blanket, or sweater," I ask, "that you could easily buy at the store?"

"To be totally honest, I don't know. I try to explain it, mostly to nonknitters, to get nonknitters to understand what the appeal of knitting is. Because I get this question all the time, the kind of affectionate, joking, trying-not-to-humiliate-me-while-humiliating-me kind of question. People that I used to work with who say, 'It looks like such a repetitive, mindless activity. Why do you do this?'

"There's mindless knitting, of course, which is good for watching TV. But I don't know if it's a chicken-or-an-egg thing. Did I need to be doing something with my hands while I was watching TV before I became a knitter? That's what mindless knitting is for me. I like that feeling of having something going in my hands when I have to sit still. When I'm in a waiting room, when I'm on an airplane, if I don't have something to knit, it's physically and psychologically difficult for me. So that could be OCD. But I don't think I was like that before I became a knitter. I think knitting became a comforting activity for me.

"I used to do crossword puzzles a lot. In the *New York Times*, the crossword puzzle is a different level of difficulty each day of the week. I was always a Thursday kind of person. The Monday puzzle was too much of a snooze. It wasn't enough fun. It was almost a race to see how fast you could get the letters in. Sunday could be a nightmare. In the Will Shortz era, I get all of the cultural references, so the Sunday is easier for me than it was. It used to be really hard. When it was Eugene Maleska, forget about it.

"Friday was always a hard one. Those were good puzzles because your mind was working but there was a kind of relaxation in it, a kind of rhythm. To me, there's a lot of thinking in knitting. But it's a nonverbal thinking, which I think is relaxing for people who live a very verbal life. And most people in professional jobs live by words. The meaning of words is always what they're dealing with in their work life. So I think that's it for me. The fact that there are solvable puzzles, solvable problems in knitting."

Kay holds up part of the sweater in her lap. When she knits, she pulls her glasses down to the end of her nose and looks over them at the work in her hands.

"I'm reknitting an Aran pullover right now that I knit five years ago. This sounds really weird, but after I started the chart, I remembered certain things about it. They came back to me in a nonverbal way. It's not really muscle memory, but some deep recess in your brain that goes 'I remember that, when I'm working the diamond in the pattern, the double moss that I changed from knit to purl on the right side and is not on the wrong side.' It keeps me just engaged enough that it's not boring, but it's not rocket science either. I can't do it when I'm tired. I can't do it when my mind is not sharp. That to me is the best I can do to describe what's pleasant about it.

"You'll finish the Starmore sweater and know that it's not about wearing it. It's about making it. I think that's the first step of answering why I do this. Because I like to do it. It's like Matisse—not to compare oneself to Matisse—but I just read his biography and it was so interesting to me that everywhere he went, he painted. And whether life sucked or life was great, he painted. And whether his family liked it or not, he painted. It was just something that he did. I really think it must be a similar thing, for those of us who do not have that kind of artistic talent. We can knit."

But there's more to why knitters knit, Kay thinks.

"There's all the other stuff that people talk about, the hearthy, homey, cozy part of it. People talk about knitting their thoughts into something they're making for somebody. I do love to make things for people. I think I have some—in my own pretentious mind—some more sophisticated version of knitting prayers into something. But when somebody is having some kind of crisis, I often find myself knitting them something. It's like making a casserole."

We sit in silence for a minute and watch Michael Phelps swim in a preliminary heat and kibitz about whether he'll complete his quest for fourteen gold medals. I wonder aloud, again, "If I complete my quest, which is finishing this sweater in less than a year, will I actually have a Starmore when I'm done, given that I've been using different yarn?"

"Probably not," Kay says. "A Chanel suit is a Chanel suit. And I think that's what Starmore is like. It's only a Starmore if you use her yarn and you do her thing. You don't change anything about it. If I were going to make one, that's what I would do, partly for the exercise of doing it. Also, authenticity is important to me.

"My one Kaffe Fassett sweater is the one everybody calls the de-Kaffe because it's like Kaffe-lite. It's striped, so it's one color per row. It's in cotton but it's in very hot colors, reds and purples and burgundies. This was back in the days when every six months the Rowan magazine would come out and I would obligatory-knit at least one thing from that magazine. It was 'What am I going to knit?' not 'If I'm going to knit.'

"A lot of other people were making it too. It was a cute little raglan cardigan, unlike any shape that I'd ever seen him do. Other people were going, 'Well, I don't like these reds. I don't look good in red.' So they were changing all of the colors of these twelve-color stripes. I was like, that is nuts. It's like changing the colors in a Matisse. It's a striped cardigan. The only reason you're knitting it is because Kaffe told you how to put these colors together. I was a fundamentalist about that. I think with that sweater I was right."

Kay pauses for a second, pushing her glasses back up on her nose.

"But then with a lot of knitted patterns, it just doesn't matter," Kay says, slowly. "They're so utilitarian or so trendy." Kay puts some Elizabeth Zimmerman designs in that utilitarian category. "She certainly exhorts people to individualize, yet some of her patterns are just so instantly recognizable."

One of Zimmerman's best-known patterns is the Baby Surprise Jacket. The surprise isn't the baby; it's Zimmerman's construction. The pattern has you knit a squarish amoeboid shape that you'd swear could never fit a human, not even a baby one. But if you follow her instructions, the "Wow!" moment comes when you stitch the seams. Somehow, you end up with a cute little sweater. It's a pattern you can do in almost any yarn, with just a few adjustments.

"No matter what you do to it, it's going to be very recognizable and very authentic. That's brilliant to me," Kay says.

"As she grew older, Julia Child evolved to simplifying and streamlining her recipes, but she never evolved to saying, 'Here's my idea of how to make this, and you just go,' like Nigel Slater and Nigella Lawson are always telling you. If you're going to make the boeuf bourguignon, you're going to make a little *x* on the bottom of every onion. Why are you doing that? Because that is what you do."

In Kay's view, Julia Child was right to be so strict about it, because if she weren't, then "everything would taste like tuna casserole. It was important to say, 'This is the way French cooking is done.' As everybody became better cooks, it was then okay to give people permission."

But, according to Kay, sometimes you can apply your fundamentalism to the wrong action.

"Later in Child's life there was this whole craze for Mediterranean food, and she was always, like, 'Italian food? Why would you eat it?' And she was wrong. She was just absolutely wrong. It was a failing for her to not realize that there could be more than one true faith," Kay says.

I wonder if Child would have come around if she'd hooked up with Cyndi and done some yoga. I also wonder if Starmore believes that hers is the one true faith.

The next morning, Kay walks me to Knitty City, her local yarn shop in Manhattan, and we promise to see each other at the annual Rhinebeck festival. At the shop I pick up another skein of Colinette Jitterbug in Copperbeech, which is, sadly, a different dye lot. If nothing else, the skein from New York can sit on my shelf with the skein from Nashville and talk about knitting. If I hear them start doing Tammy Wynette numbers, however, it might be time for me to lie down for a bit.

When Lana and I get home from our jaunt to the bright lights of the big city, daughter Maddy flings herself into my arms. There is nothing better than a kid's hug.

After dinner, I settle in on the couch, pull Lana and all her balls of yarn and the chart out of my tote bag. I shake out everything that has collected at the bottom, which includes an unused tissue, a metro card, a paper clip, half a croissant, and a hotel room key card. Maddy traces one of the fleurs-de-lis on the sweater's front.

"Hey, Mom," she says. "This is pretty. Can you put these on my hat?"

Oh. Rats. The hat.

"Sure, sweet pea. You'll have it by the winter."

Note to self: Make hat.

7

September and October

Further Travels with Mary Tudor

Two-day pass to the New York State Sheep and Wool Festival in Rhinebeck: $15

Rhinebeck, aka the New York State Sheep and Wool Festival, is like Mardi Gras but without people shouting "Show us your tits!" You can think of it as your ten-year high school reunion, provided you went to a high school with twelve thousand students. Rhinebeck is always the third weekend in October at the Dutchess County Fairgrounds.

The *New York Times*'s Tina Kelley captures Rhinebeck most accurately in her 2007 story. "If every sense has its slaking place—a museum gallery for the eyes, a four-star restaurant for the taste buds, a concert for the ears—the sense of touch has the New York State Sheep and Wool Festival at the Dutchess County Fairgrounds. With a dozen barns filled with fiber merchants and countless cages of mohair and cashmere goats and Angora rabbits, this weekend was a celebration of the tactile. Even people on the midway occasionally petted the shawled shoulders of strangers."

But the weekend is about more than touching fibers, it's also about reconnecting with the knitting community. On these usually crisp fall days, knitters (and crocheters and spinners too) step out of their houses and rub yarns. The exceedingly polite Knitterazzi stalk authors like Ann, Kay, and Stephanie. We feel like we know them, of course, having read their blogs for so long.

More than 275 vendor booths fill the fairground and mostly sell the materials, like yarn, needles, carders, and spinning wheels, to make other items. One vendor sells little felted gnomes that become the darling of the online forums. A few vendors cater to the shepherds who are exhibiting their hoof stock and sell flea dip and troughs. The smell of standard fair food—think protein on a stick that has been battered and deep-fried—mixes with more upscale offerings created by students from the nearby Culinary Institute of America.

In the early 1970s, if you'd asked the organizers what the festival would look like in thirty-five years, I can't imagine that they would have been able to envision the popularity it has achieved. Even in the last few years—I first went in 2003—the number of fairgoers has grown exponentially. In 2008 the number of attendees made it nearly impossible to walk from booth to booth without accidentally groping a stranger's yarn.

While I was in Pittsburgh, Trish and I had made plans to go to Rhinebeck. She drove up to my house on the night before the festival started. From there, we drove another two hours southeast through the mountains to get to Kingston, New York, which is where the closest hotel with a vacant room was. A third college pal, Quinn, drove down from her house near Bath, Maine.

When Trish and I get to the Holiday Inn, we're both a little bleary from the drive, which wound up being thirty minutes longer than expected because of an unexpected detour. It turns out that bridges are important when crossing a river, and the one that we needed had been washed out during the last big rain in these parts. Trish and I are both from the city of bridges. Yet the idea of miles and miles of road suddenly becoming inaccessible because of one bridge took both of us by surprise.

I still find it hard to wrap my head around the fact that I have known Quinn and Trish for more than half my life. I also find it hard to deal with the fact that we are all almost forty, the age at which your options start to diminish because you are more or less locked into a life path. I read somewhere—and one of the signs of getting older is that I can no longer remember where—that life is shaped like a diamond. At the start, your choices are few. They get greater and greater with each year until forty or so, when the choices you've made start to limit the ones you can make—until you die, which is generally as much of a choice as being born is.

I don't find this bleak, actually. I'm fairly content with the choices I've made and the ones I'm not at ease with are minor. The knowledge that my diamond is getting narrower just makes me more careful about my time and likely to enjoy where I am more. Besides, I'm tired of deciding and, in a way, welcome having less big stuff to think about. Your mileage, of course, may vary.

Even harder to have predicted is that all three of us would be knitters, and not just knitters but knitters who would deeply dig spending a weekend at a sheep and wool festival.

(For the record, I tried to convince a fourth former roommate to join us. She is not a knitter, nor does she aspire to be one. She did admit that getting together sounded like fun but that she would rather spend the weekend, say, cleaning out her gutters rather than looking at miles of yarn and ruminants. I don't take this personally, since she is an environmental chemist and I can't imagine going to a festival devoted to sediment and water, which seems to be the focus of her research.)

Despite our all having gone to the same liberal arts college, the three of us have taken different life paths. Quinn, who has red hair in a buzz cut and is decorated with tattoos of her own design, is homeschooling two kids deep in the wilds of a tidal island. She's a former children's librarian and eats only raw foods. These are not the choices that I would make—the idea of spending that much time with my kids alone puts me right off my fully cooked lunch—but for her, they are absolutely perfect.

Trish, who went on to get a master's degree in English by writing her thesis about Virginia Woolf's *The Waves*, has always been the most deliberate of the three of us. She got married just a few years ago. So far, she's been focused on career rather than kids, although by the time you read this, we may all be knitting her some bootees. And while I would love to tell you what she does, I have to admit that I don't understand it. It involves colleges and words and public relations and computer databases. Your guess is as good as mine.

My life-management technique of flailing around until I hit on something that works would make Trish nuts. My reluctance to embrace the spirituality of the natural world wouldn't fly in Quinn's house. And yet when I'm with the two of them, I feel more at peace with myself.

As a bonus, they both make the appropriate noises when I pull Lana out of her bag. I'm up to the shoulders, the second of which I'm about to graft together with a Kitchener stitch. We're in the hotel room the next evening, collapsed on our respective beds (or, in Quinn's case, rollaway) and knitting. There are gatherings of knitters all over the Holiday Inn and you run into knots of them when you leave your room to get ice. There are knitters in the restaurant, knitters in the lounge, and knitters in the lobby. It's a refreshing sight.

The three of us had made grand plans to hit the Ravelry party up the road in Red Hook that night but can't summon the energy to move. I'd like to say that this is a big change from college and allege that we'd party into the wee hours but that would be a big fat lie. Our group was more likely to lose track of time while playing euchre and debating the nature of God. Yes, we were that geeky. And pretentious—but mostly geeky. Since there are only three of us, we can't play euchre. Rather than God or our lack of belief in the same, we talk about what we saw. Quinn maps out her plan of attack for the next day because she's hot on the trail of some gloves. Trish and I tell Quinn about the sheepdog trials we watched during lunch, and if you ever want to see a pure expression of joy, watch a well-trained border collie or Australian shepherd herding sheep.

Trish is playing with her new hand-carved nostepinne, which is a Scandinavian tool for winding center-pull yarn balls from unwound hanks of yarn, which are almost impossible to knit directly from. The cardboard cores of toilet paper rolls can also be used to achieve the same effect but are less aesthetically satisfying.

As I Kitchener, I profess my love for the fairground's restroom attendants, who not only turn a necessity into a pleasure by keeping the line moving and the sinks tidy, but also put on a show with their constant patter. "If you got to go," one attendant will shout as she points you to the open stall, "let it flow."

But what we mostly talk about are all the knitted items we saw. We refer to them by their pattern names, like "I saw four February Ladies in the fried artichoke line" or "I lost count of all the Clapotis." We're not the only ones doing it. Strangers stop each other by yelling the name of the garment, like, "Nice Mr. Greenjeans! Did you use Miss Priss?" The wonderful part is that no one needs to explain what that means.

I don't spot any Mary Tudors, but marvel at some examples of Anne of Cleves and Elizabeth I. I also see a lot of women who hug and kvell at seeing each other again. Because I'm an eavesdropper, I figure out that most of them keep tabs on each other through their blogs during the other 360+ days of the year. For a few, this is the first time they've met in person someone they'd describe as a close friend but have known only through email and virtual forums. The intersection between newfangled technology and knitters' deep-seated need for community never fails to surprise me.

As we're walking back to Quinn's car on the second day of the festival, I plow into one of my own friends from the Internet. Quite a few of those iconic patterns, like Pomatomus, Calorimetry, and Ice Queen (which litter the festival like the autumn leaves that are dropping from the trees), were first published in *Knitty*. A few weeks ago, I'd just gotten back from visiting with Amy R. Singer, the visionary behind Knitty.com, in Toronto.

I was in Toronto to find my knitting mojo. The work on Lana's body was going so very slowly that, to the naked eye, it appeared to have stopped. Actually, it more than appeared that way. For six weeks, the tote bag had barely left the chair that it was lounging in. Even when I moved Lana, it wasn't because I was going to work on it but because the cat was sleeping on it. My ennui was so severe that I'd taken up cross-stitch again and completed a long-avoided sampler.

If the knitting universe can be said to have a point around which everything revolves, that center would be Toronto. Not only is it home to Singer, it's also where Pearl-McPhee and designers Kate Gilbert, Fiona Ellis, and Dorothy Siemens rest their needles. Wannietta Prescod, the three-time World's Fastest Knitter, lives in Toronto, as does knitting visionary Debbie New. Toronto is also home to the Textile Museum of Canada and the Needle Arts Book Shop.

If that doesn't convince you, there are about the same number of yarn shops in Toronto, where 2.5 million people live, as in New York City, which has a population of 8.2 million people. To quote Pearl-McPhee from *Vogue Knitting*'s fall 2008 story on the knitters in the North, "The amount of knitting you see here is an ordinary event. It's not Worldwide Knit in Public Day; it's not a guild function. It's just Tuesday, and you're not the only one knitting on the subway."

If the city itself doesn't give my mojo a nudge, the women I'm visiting should. There's Singer, of course, but I'm also meeting the Yarn Harlot for an early dinner and knitting.

I'd dropped off my still-hatless elder child with her grandmother in Rochester, New York, then drove over to Buffalo the next morning. I crossed the border at Lewiston/Queenston. It was a near thing, however, and I briefly wondered if I'd have to call my mother-in-law to come bail me out of a Canadian jail.

The trouble started when I pulled up to the guard. I handed my passport to him. Yes, I know that a U.S. citizen technically doesn't have to show a passport to cross this border. I get to use my passport so infrequently, however, that I use it every place I can.

"Where are you from?" the guard politely asks.

There's a long pause on my part. It's still early enough that not all the parts of my brain that control speech have been soaked in coffee yet. Plus, I am not driving with my children, which means I haven't had to process anyone's speaking at me for an hour.

"Um . . . Oneonta, New York," I say, at the same moment

that I realize that my passport probably has my old address on it. Later investigation will prove that my passport doesn't have any address on it, but again, I was undercaffeinated.

"Where are you going?" he asks.

"Toronto."

"Why?"

I start to say, "To find my knitting mojo," but realize he is already starting to have some doubts about my trustworthiness. As am I, come to think of it.

"To visit," I say.

"Who?"

"Stephanie."

He looks at me, then steps out of his little booth so that he can walk around to the back of my minivan. The fact that I'm driving a minivan should be enough of a clue that I'm relatively harmless.

"What's her last name?" he asks.

"McPhee. Or Pearl. I'm not really sure which is technically her *last* last name."

"How do you know her?"

Again, I start to say, "She's the Yarn Harlot. Everybody knows her." But don't. What I say instead might not have been a better choice. "We're both knitters."

The guard looks at me, blandly polite, but I get the sense that he's weighing his options, like he's wondering if pepper spray or a bash to the head is a better way to subdue me. The fact that those two choices are the first that leap to my mind prove that I would be a very bad Canadian.

He looks at my passport. "How long are you staying?"

"Until Thursday."

"Do you have anything to declare, besides clothes and personal items?"

I start to say, "Yarn."

"No," I say instead.

"Welcome to Canada. Enjoy your stay."

I went on to make a half dozen wrong turns, almost all of which were the result of listening to a radio show about Mark Bittman's no-knead bread, which I love but can't imagine talking about for more than a minute or two. These two women had deeply held opinions on it, which fascinated me for over thirty minutes. I was so engrossed that I missed my turn, then missed it again after turning around.

A few hours later, I arrived at the Purple Purl, a yarn shop on Queen Street East. In navigating there from my hotel, I discovered two things: folks look at you strangely when you call a streetcar a trolley, and Coffee Crisp candy bars may be my destroyer. Not only are the Canadians kicking my country's ass when it comes to knitting, they are also doing the same when it comes to mass-produced confections.

I'm meeting Amy at the Purple Purl's traditional Tuesday knit night. The chairs in the yarn-packed store fill quickly. Amy, who has short black hair with a red streak in the front, breezes in shortly after I manage to explain who I am and why I'm there. She's about five four and is, as she'd say so herself, a big girl. She's not obese by any stretch of the imagination but larger around than average, especially in the chest area. And as one who is also amply proportioned, I know a mighty rack when I see one.

Amy comes bearing gifts. Lorna's Laces, an indie yarn dyer in Chicago, has worked up three samples of the colorway that Amy has designed. She'd like to see some of them knitted into swatches before settling on the final blend. One problem—the base yarn is wool and Amy is allergic to it.

So the hanks are balled up and distributed. I borrow a pair of small-enough needles—I foolishly left all my tiny needles at home—and work up a square while we talk.

Amy learned to knit when she was six but wasn't what she calls a "knitter-knitter" until college. It's only in the last three or four years that she stopped slavishly following patterns.

For years, Amy quilted. One of the reasons she returned to the needles, however, was for the fiber.

"Yarn is really sexy," Amy says. "Silk is a perfect example. I don't know if I could afford to buy a silk sweater, but I can knit one. It's still going to be less expensive and I get to play with the silk the whole time. A lot of the stuff I want to buy uses fibers I can't wear.

"I also like knitting as a good Zen-out thing. I pick the mellowest thing I can, zone into it, and just go," she says.

Speaking of Zen knitting, I'm so focused on my swatch—the combination of black, gray, and almost turquoise is one of my favorite colorways ever—I almost forget that I'm talking to Amy for a reason. I'm finally to the point with Mary Tudor that I'm not scared of the colorwork. In fact, the opposite is starting to happen: I'm a little bored by it. But I still want to know if there are projects that frighten accomplished knitters.

"Anything Kaffe Fassett does scares me," Amy says. "I

get two balls of yarn and the tangling makes me so crabby I can't imagine how anybody works with more than two balls of yarn. If I had to do anything, it would be Fair Isle. But intarsia scares the crap out of me. In some ways, if you look at what Kaffe does, it really is appealing, but there is a certain threshold over which I am not willing to go."

"What is the hardest project you've ever taken on? *Hard* can be defined however you want."

"I think I have to say I'm still in the middle of it. The very first thing I ever knit as a grown-up was a cabled vest, which turned out to be a piece of cake. So the thing I thought would be hard was not hard. What seems to be hard is this sweater that is out of the *No Sheep* book, the cabled cardigan, which is knitted to about here," Amy says, as she indicates her midsection. *No Sheep for You*, a book about nonwool yarns and patterns, is one of the books Amy has edited. Also on her résumé are *Big Girl Knits*, *More Big Girl Knits*, and *Knit Wit*.

Amy can't say why the cabled cardigan stopped. "It took me forever to get to this point, and now that I've broken past the underarm, all of a sudden it just feels like I'll never finish it. It's not physically that hard. But it's not mindless. I can't just sit and knit. I have to constantly know where I am in the pattern. For me, that's difficult. It takes away the Zen."

I know what she means. Without my self-imposed deadline, I can easily see myself tossing Mary Tudor on the Knitting Closet Shelf of Shame, which is where all unfinished knitwear goes. It's like my own island of misfit toys, stuffed full of projects that I've either royally screwed up or lack the drive to finish. The last hat I started for Maddy—out of a garish pink soy-based yarn that looked fun—is jammed in there too, mocking me.

If I were a stronger person, I'd clean it out and recycle the yarn. But to do that would be to admit defeat, and I will not be defeated by my knitting. Instead, I'll ignore it. Who needs an exit plan when turning a blind eye will do?

Like so many knitters, Amy usually has a couple of projects going at any given time.

"I have this ongoing tube that's made out of lace-weight that will never end, and when it ends, I'll start a new one. The goal of that is not to finish it, it's just to keep it so that I can knit it everywhere," Amy says. "I just finished one sweater and another sweater, and that pink cable thing is still in the basket. I have to finish it because it's going to be beautiful. So, usually a sweater and a couple of things. And maybe something I'm designing, but not often."

When Amy does design, which isn't as often as she'd like, she's drawn to keeping her patterns simple.

"There are all of these things that are automatically eliminated. I want to keep the pattern so that you have a 'break' row. And I want to make it so that it looks really good with variegated yarn. If you took a look at my patterns, it's what I call Amy's Mindless Knitting." She explains that she tries to make her own designs, such as Tuscany, a lace scarf in *No Sheep*, beginner-friendly. "Every decision that I made was based on making it easy. That actually makes the project harder for me to design, but once you get into it, oh, my God, is it ever great," Amy says.

I dig out Lana; yes, I have it with me because I keep hoping that the Torontonian air will make me want to knit another row. There are oohs and aahs from the other knitters, one of whom, Emily Way, is also a Starmore junkie.

"Have there been any projects that you've been actually scared of? Or do you just choose to not knit them?" I ask Amy.

"I'm really careful to choose things that don't scare me too badly. I don't think I ever would have picked up Charlotte's Web until a friend showed me the tricks to knitting that specific lace scarf. It's a really easy lace shawl once you understand the basic rules," Amy says.

"If you take a look online, you'll see spreadsheets from people trying to figure out how many repeats are left. It couldn't be any simpler, but to get the concept in their heads they've gone all the way to China and back, instead of just looking around the corner. Someone showed me how to go around the corner; otherwise that might have seemed like the most difficult thing I ever did."

When researching Starmore's sweaters, I brazenly stole the technique of marking up my own graphs with lines every five stitches so that I can keep track of where I am. Had another Starmore knitter not mentioned it on Ravelry, I never would have thought of it. Now I can't imagine working without my red lines.

"Do you think most knitting gets down to 'It's easy if you know the trick'?" I ask.

"No," Amy says. "I think you have to pick carefully. When I'm picking a lace pattern to design or to knit, I want something that has a purl-back row. That eliminates many of the most beautiful lace patterns. So no, not everything is going to be simple. For example, on my wall is the pattern for Ann Hanson's Bee Fields shawl. That is probably going to be the most complicated thing I will ever knit. It's not a pattern I've designed. I love how it looks. I don't think there are any purl-back rows. I don't know. I just bought it not knowing how complicated it might be. It has not even been cast on, but it's there. It's gonna happen."

It's reassuring to know that even Amy Singer has patterns that she loves but feels intimidated by. She has become a knitting visionary, hitting the knitting spotlight not for her designs but for her entrepreneurial spirit. When she first published *Knitty*, the idea of an online knitting magazine hadn't even been dreamed of, much less tested. Once again, necessity proves to be the best inspiration for a knitter.

"I knit when I was little and there were little pattern books, flyers and things," Amy says. "Then I knit when I was in college and there were bigger books and some flyers. This was what you could choose from. You'd have to wait until the next one came out or the next *Vogue Knitting* came out. They wouldn't have designs in my size or stuff that would only fit an average-shaped body," Amy says.

Our concept of a community of knitters is a relatively new one, especially for those who live somewhere without a yarn shop or fall outside the shop's demographic. If no one in your family knew how to knit, it used to be hard to find a place to go for help.

"The fact is, in the eighties, if you got bored or stuck, you might have stopped knitting. If you got stuck in a hard spot or challenged beyond your level of ability or even just intimidated, even though it may not have been hard, there was almost no place to go unless you had an experienced knitter sitting next to you or could go to your grandmother. Or you would have to go and ask the yarn store lady for help. I remember the first time I asked someone for help and was like nineteen or twenty. I asked her to show me how to do cables. I felt like it was a big deal to go in and have her teach me how to do cables. It was just so isolating."

None of that is true anymore. "There's constant support. Even in the late 1990s, when the Internet was just catching on, I was still quilting then and I saw the support quilters were giving to each other on just simple forums or mailing lists. That was new. Then places like the Purple Purl started to open up, partially, I think, because people on the Internet demand this kind of place to hang out. You want an atmosphere where you feel like it's family, and if you need help, there's someone there to help you. And that's all due to the Internet. All of it," Amy says.

Knitty was a big part of that too, for more knitters than Amy could know. Discovering Knitty.com was such a watershed moment for me that I can remember exactly where I was, a cubicle in the newsroom of the paper I wrote for in Knoxville, Tennessee. I can't recall the story I was supposed to be working on, but I can remember the moment when issue three's front page loaded and I saw designer Bonne Marie Burns's Sitcom Chic sweater. The garment itself was fresh, like it was designed by someone who was close to my age. The sweater patterns at my local yarn shop looked downright frumpy and grannyish by comparison. But the best part about

Knitty was—and still is—its attitude. It is unapologetic about loving the craft, despite its fusty reputation. The online magazine has been great for Amy as well as for younger knitters.

"What has been the most gratifying part of *Knitty*?" I ask.

"Getting to quit my day job really does not suck," Amy says. "For knitting as a craft, I think we helped change some stuff, which is kind of nice."

"There are people—maybe they would be designing now anyway—who I was coaxing to submit. I'd say, 'Send patterns in and we'll publish them!' Especially at the beginning, almost nobody got rejected because so few things came in, and when they did come in, most were pretty good. Eventually it got to the point where we had to start saying no. It's given people a place to show that they can be creative and they don't have to be Kaffe Fassett to get published. For example, we have fifteen-year-old high school kids who design really good socks," Amy says.

Amy loves editing *Knitty*. "I wish we could do more and bigger. I wish that I had enough money that I could hire staff, have an assistant, and have someone consistently there to make sure all of the little loose ends were taken care of."

My swatch is done, as are the other two. We hold them all together and quickly eliminate one. That one is pretty, mind you, but the two that remain are prettier. The sample that I swatched—evocatively named "B"—winds up being the winner. Amy, bless her, lets me keep the sample skeins, which I eventually work up into a Clapotis, which is one of Knitty.com's iconic scarf patterns. You can't go to a yarn festival without seeing at least a dozen "clappers."

But right now, I'm still focused on Mary Tudor.

"Here's the question I'm still trying to answer for myself. Since I'm in a room full of knitters, it seems like the right place to ask it. Given that I am not following Alice Starmore's pattern exactly, what exactly will I have when I'm done?"

Emily, the other Starmore lover in the room, says, "A sweater that you wear and that you don't tell her about." The dozen people in the circle laugh.

"My answer is a little different," Amy says, "because I wrote to Alice Starmore before the Internet was too big a deal. It was 2001, maybe? I wrote and I said, 'I really love your patterns but I can't touch wool. What do you suggest?' Her response came back: 'I suggest you don't knit our sweaters.'

"But it wasn't said in a mean way. She just said, 'We don't think there is any way you can achieve this sweater without using wool yarn.' So, honestly, I never tried. I know there are yarns I can use that won't give me the result that I want. The fact that I can't touch wool gives me an extra reason not to really care what she has to say. I can appreciate her design gorgeousness," Amy concedes, mentioning that the cabled designs like St. Brigid are her favorites. "I think they would look horrible on me but, my God, they're beautiful."

As much as I love knit night at the Purple Purl, the following night's knit night at Lettuce Knit is the most fun I've had in quite some time. The fault the first night was mine, most likely. At the Purl, I was having a hard time shaking the white line fugue, which has nothing to do with anything illegal and everything to do with what my brain does when I drive alone for long distances. I love taking solo road trips but always forget that it's best if I don't have to interact with other people until I've had a decent night's sleep.

After a post-Purl dinner at the Peter Pan Bistro, where I had the stunning realization that smoking is still permitted in restaurants in an otherwise lovely country, and a long hot shower in my hotel room, which had been aggressively tidied, I fell into the deep sleep of the virtuous.

(As a mom with two small kids myself, I include the above description as sleep porn for my tired sisters. For the money shot, I got up to pee in the middle of the night and didn't step on a single Lego or Polly Pocket shoe. You may now bask in the afterglow.)

Perhaps my mood could be chalked up to nine hours of delightful rest, but I laughed so hard at Lettuce Knit that my face was still sore the next day. There was also beer involved, but I don't think correlation and causation are the same here.

It also had nothing to do with feeling up one of the hosts. She was just a willing visual aid for a story about my older child, who has taken to laying her hands on various parts of my body (my left breast was the most recent target), usually when I'm fresh out of the shower and defenseless, and saying "flap, flap, flap" while she waggles my saggy skin back and forth. Denny, a person I instantly loved, offered up her own boobal area, and the rest, as they say, is history.

Denny also kept pushing me to learn to spin. She had a variety of tactics for plying her skills, including the phrase,

"First one is free." But I stuck firm in my conviction that I can only handle one obsession at one time. Until Mary Tudor is completed, all my focus needs to be directed at her. There also isn't any room in my house for spinning-related paraphernalia like wheels and whorls and fleece. When I have more room, I will delve into the alchemy of turning dirty animal fluff into gorgeous yarn.

Maybe I was just won over by Denny because she said that, for an American, "I talked normal." Which says either something about my lack of an accent because I've moved so much or that Canadians all expect us to talk like our former Whistleass-in-Chief. Regardless, it was a pleasure to do my small part to assure our neighbors to the north that some of us do know the English language and how it can be put together.

The morning had started auspiciously. I trapped myself in my hotel room on purpose, because I had a freelance writing project that absolutely had to get done, even if I wanted to go out and explore the city. Sometimes it sucks to be an adult.

My reward came later, however. Stephanie Pearl-McPhee and I met up for coffee and yarn shopping in the early afternoon, with dinner and knitting to follow. Don't tell my husband, but it was as close to a perfect date as I've had. Perhaps it was because neither of us was going to try to lure the other to my hotel room afterward and the pressure was off.

Or it could be because we went to Romni Wools, which is as close to yarn store nirvana as you can get without actually dying. Just walking through the doors gave me the vapors. I almost sat down to put my head between my knees.

Every direction you look, there is yarn from floor to ceiling. Not just any yarn, mind, but good yarn, the kind of yarn that makes grown women weep. The basement—oh, the basement—is a bargain hunter's paradise, where heaps of fine yarn are marked down for no discernible reason. I didn't spend much time down there, however, because my mind was already reeling from the first floor.

Stephanie, who is short enough that I can't spot her wildly curly hair over the tops of the aisles, was on the hunt for the makings of Hey, Teach, a *Knitty* pattern that she was consumed by. I was on the hunt for nothing in particular but still found plenty to spend my money on, like Norwegian yarn for some Fair Isle mittens with a squirrel motif that I wanted to knit for the college friend who didn't come to Rhinebeck. I also buy some funky green and brown sock yarn and a set of sock-yarn-sized needles, not because I need them but because all of mine are at home and I need to cast on for a sock *right now*.

Also in the bag is a button that I couldn't resist, which the woman behind the counter tells me reminds her of a licorice allsort. I look at her blankly. "I don't know what that is," I say. She explains that it's a candy, you know, you buy them in a tin and they come with other shapes of licorice?

I still have no idea what she's talking about, assume it's a Canadian thing, and move on. (Later I see licorice allsorts in my grocery, which means it's not a Canadian thing—and again proves that one shouldn't assume—but my ignorance is a byproduct of my own hatred of licorice. Coffee Crisp still beats the heinie off all American candy bar technology. That is a proven fact and not a mere assumption.)

Once we leave Romni, which I eventually have to do as an

act of self-preservation, we head out for Italian food, walking through Toronto's textile district. We pass half a dozen fabric stores and notions shops. It's an easy walk and not just because the city is fairly flat and the weather is pleasant. Stephanie's love for her city is infectious. Listening to her talk about it is a pleasure.

We luck into a window seat at an Italian restaurant, where the spinach gnocchi are good and the pizza margarita even better. We talk about—what else?—knitting.

"I have been knitting since I was four years old," Stephanie says. "I remember the day with enormous precision. I remember what the weather was. I remember what I was wearing. I remember what my grandmother was wearing. I remember the color of the wool. I remember where we were. I remember everything about that moment. I've said it before. I remember everything about that moment the way that I have heard other people describe religious epiphanies."

"What color was the wool?" I ask.

"Yellow," she replies, with no hesitation. "It was a beautiful day. The sun was shining. We were sitting in the shade. There were bees—I still remember all the bees on all the flowers. The smell of the roses behind me. And my grandmother was wearing a green and white paisley housedress. Except for the housedress, I thought it was a really elegant moment.

"I remember walking into the back garden. They had a very traditional English-style garden. So there was the house and then you came down a little hill and there were tall English flowerbeds with roses all the way around and a big tree that gave shade. The garden came around and there was an archway, then a further garden beyond that. My grandmother was sitting in the further garden, in a chair.

"I came running out of the house, down the hill, through the front garden, into the back garden, and I said, 'Nana, Nana, guess what? I learned how to read.' She looked at me and she said, 'Well, if you can do something as hard as read, then you can do something as simple as knit. Sit beside me.' She showed me how to cast on, cast off, knit, and purl. I remember thinking that this was very important. I wasn't sure why or how, I just knew that I had learned something really significant."

Unlike for most of the knitters I know, the connection between Stephanie and the craft was immediate.

"I knew that this was something that was fascinating for me the first time I met it," she says. "I'd seen my nana knit for years. She was always knitting. She was a professional knitter, so she knit morning, noon, and night. It'd never occurred to me that it was interesting. I thought it was like sleeping. It was just something somebody was doing.

"I knit a yellow acrylic potholder. My mother used it until the early eighties, when she melted it in a fairly horrific kitchen incident that we don't speak of. It may or may not have been intentional. It was a pretty ratty-looking potholder by then, but I had very significant emotional feelings about that potholder."

"Do you have any yarn in the stash from that time?" I ask.

"A tiny little bit. I have none from when I was a child because when I was really little—you know, children don't have jobs, so all of your yarn is gift yarn. Or hand-me-down yarn. Or yarn that grown-ups hate. You get all the shite. I only have a few balls that are left," she says. "I'm pretty good about culling the stash."

"So what's the appeal of knitting?" I ask.

"I think about that a lot. It's really not that interesting. If you just look at what's happening, you're pulling a loop through another loop. That's all you do. You can do it frontwards. You can do it backwards. You can put your yarn over the needle. You can knit two together, and I believe I've just covered all of the executions. Different combinations—but that's pretty much it. It shouldn't be this gripping to me," Stephanie says. "I love the continuous nature of it. I love that it takes so long to make an object that can be undone by pulling on one string. Isn't that compelling?"

There's something about the impermanence of handmade things that speaks to me as well. Mass-produced plastic crap will be floating in the oceans long after I'm dead, long after even my great-grandchildren are dead. But a knitted item, like a sock or a dishrag, can be easily returned to its simplest state with just one tug. They are ephemeral, knitted goods, like the sandpaintings of Tibetan monks, who sweep them away after their creation is done.

"I love that it is an act of transformation. I love that you're taking one thing and turning it into another thing. I love that that thing could be anything. I love that I decide. I love that in order to knit you have to do something right thousands of times. You can congratulate yourself all of those times. Knitting's very good for your self-esteem."

In *Free-Range Knitter*, the essay "Rachel" is about a friend of Stephanie's knitting herself through a bleak period in her life by tackling a seemingly impossible afghan. From the piece, it's clear that this project was Rachel's life raft; the work kept her spirits buoyed enough to carry her back to safety. Some knit blankets in times of stress; others knit hats. Knitting is good for your mental health too, I mention.

"I also like that I am making something useful. I've always felt that knitted things met the gold standard for human objects, that they were both beautiful and useful. And I'm intrigued by it. The more I learn about it, the more I'm interested," she says. "I don't just mean the more I learn to do lace or do cables, I mean the more I find out what's happening in your brain when you knit. You use both hemispheres at once. I find it absolutely gripping that knitting really is changing the way your brain and body work for the rest of your life. Knitters are different from other people."

We both pause for a minute to let that sink in: knitters' brains are different from those of nonknitters. The same can be said, I'd imagine, about golfers or quilters too, but they already get enough press.

"What's the hardest project you've ever tackled?" I ask.

"The hardest project I ever tackled was an afghan for my brother and his intended for their wedding. I've written about this before, but I made an attempt to show them how much I loved them with a blanket. So I made the blanket really big. Because I felt like I love them a lot, so it should be a lot of blanket," she says, spreading out her arms to show how large the blanket was.

All knitters have projects that they knit to show how much they love someone. Most knitters have dozens, frankly. I used to knit in order to show my daughter the Diva how much I loved her. I stopped, however, when she refused to wear a sweater I made for her second birthday. It was out of a purple, pink, and yellow yarn that I thought looked like clown barf but she loved. The pattern was a simple raglan that was boring to knit but, again, she loved. The end result should have been a slam dunk, a tangible reminder of how much she is loved.

Instead, she pulled it out of the box, spiked it on the floor, and ran screaming out of the room. The sweater was worn once—and then only because I bribed her with a lollipop so that I could snap just one picture of my handmade item on her person. In the photo, her face looks like she's been sucking on lemons. I did my best to chalk it up to the whims of toddlers. I'd be lying, however, if I didn't admit that I'm still just the tiniest bit hurt that my love was so despised.

Stephanie's love blanket had other issues.

"It was a color that fetched me not but was totally them. It was a pattern that fetched me not but totally was them. So the whole thing was a bit of a slog. The only thing that I had to sustain me was my love for them. I finished it in the end but not in time for the wedding. I felt really, really bummed out that I couldn't seem to pull it together; I thought that love would sustain me and it doesn't. You need knitterly entertainment. I learned a good lesson. You've got to love the yarn. You've got to love the color. Love can sustain you through a swatch. Love can sustain you through socks. But an afghan? No," she says.

"I think it was that green afghan—but only because it took stamina. Other than that, I don't want to say that I like 'hard' projects, because that sounds bad. It is only knitting and nothing bad can happen to you if you make a terrible mistake. So I figure why shouldn't you do hard stuff? The yarn is reusable. You can always pull it back and try again. It's a hobby, so wasting time doesn't matter, because frankly you're just trying to occupy yourself. It seems to me like a really safe environment to learn about challenges and making mistakes. So I don't mind hard. I do hard all of the time."

I tackled Mary Tudor in that same spirit. Advanced calculus is hard. Astrophysics is hard. Talking a toddler into wearing a sweater is hard. Knitting is easy, if only because the stakes are so low. The most tragic thing that could happen is that I start with a pile of yarn and wind up with a pile of yarn.

"That seems like an entirely attainable goal, doesn't it?" Stephanie asks. "That the worst thing that happens is that you don't get a sweater. Is that really the worst thing that could ever happen?"

Given that I don't live in Toronto, which is quickly becoming the center stitch in the modern knitting world, I don't have dozens of knitters to guide me through. I'm not sure I would have tackled Mary Tudor without seeing all the finished versions on the Internet, which prove that it can be done. In my tiny town, most of the other knitters are the ones I selfishly taught to knit so that I don't look like such a goober when I knit in public.

"I think the Internet helped us go back to a time when the things that people did were all social, because there was nothing you did on your own, without your community or without people around you who also did it. I don't think that the Internet really changed knitting in a new way. I think the Internet brought us back to an old way. I think that all it did was return knitters to a kind of community of other people who did the same thing, which is really a very old idea," Stephanie points out.

"The idea that there's only one person who knows how to knit in a community, that's new. A bunch of knitters getting together in one way or another, that's very old. I think what it did was give people communities in an unconventional way—putting you in touch with four thousand people who care about a buttonhole at three in the morning who don't have to actually be *in* your community, even though they *are* your community."

Community can be overwhelming, especially when one grows as large as the one around Stephanie's site has. I've stopped commenting on posts on her blog because I can't imagine that she can possibly read the hundreds of responses her essays get each day.

"I feel a little bit like I'm being supervised," she says. "Everything I do, there's like an opinion, a presence. Like yesterday, I showed my finished sweater saying, 'I love it. I think it's perfect.' Three or four comments down, you get the first one, somebody who says, 'I think it needs two buttons.' Next person, 'You know the button might be in the wrong place.' And the person after that, 'The button definitely goes at the bottom of the ribbing, not the top.' And the person after that says, 'It fits you wonderfully. As for the button debate . . . ' I'm like, 'Did I say there was a button debate?' But they have started a button debate of their own free will.

"It reminds me of visiting family. You say to your mother, 'Here're my new pants.' And she says, 'They're a little bit short.' And you're like, 'Did I ask you if my pants were too short? Did I ask for a judgment from you? I've already bought the pants. I'm wearing the pants.'

"I remember once my mother saying to me as I left—I was going out somewhere, very nervous, wanted to look good—and as I was leaving, my mother said to me, 'You look lovely, dear.' I said, 'Thanks, Mum.' She said, 'What's wrong with your arse?' I said, 'What do you mean, "What's wrong with your arse?"' She looks at me and she says, 'Never mind. It's probably just your pants. Have a good night.' I spent the whole night standing against a wall," Stephanie recalls.

"The Internet is like that," she continues. "There is this huge community whether you want it or not. You can't sign on for part of it. If you want the pleasure of being able to say, 'Where do you think I should put this button?' then you also have to put up with the fact that once you've decided, hundreds of people are still going to tell you your button is wrong. You have to learn how to take that the same way you learn how to take your mother's pants advice."

Stephanie has handled the pants advice with aplomb. Her mantra appears to be that you get more of what you pay attention to. Rather than focus on the irritating comments, she pays more attention to the mighty power of knitters.

"You can get them fired up about something and they will en masse go to the rescue of anyone who needs them. They form—I hate to say it because of the sheep connotation—but they form large and effective, fast-moving herds that get a great deal done very quickly. Knitters are by nature efficient, productive people or they wouldn't be knitters. You get a lot of people who are very good at getting things done, you give them a mission, and it is game over. When I said I think we should raise money for Doctors Without Borders, game over. How much would you like? Would you like that by five o'clock? No problem. You need more? I can get it for ya."

Knitters Without Borders, the not-for-profit group that sprung out of the Yarn Harlot blog, has raised over $600,000 for Doctors Without Borders in the span of two years. Stephanie's new goal is $1 million. Even her mind is boggled by the amount that knitters have raised.

Shortly after my trip up north, Stephanie's book *Free-Range Knitter* hit the *New York Times* nonfiction best-seller list. Not a "knitting" best-seller list, mind. The big list. Which makes my next question seem especially prescient.

"Did you ever expect this to happen?" I ask. "It started with an essay you posted to the knit list Yahoo! group."

"It also started because I was a freelance writer. So I was having some success in that. I'm sure you know the nightmare of freelance writing. 'You have to have six hundred words on dolphins by Friday. And make them funny.' Or 'Six hundred words on the Holocaust, but keep it light. We don't want to bring anybody down.' Or 'I need six hundred words on Rosa Parks but try not to bring race into it too much.'"

"Sounds like most of the freelance jobs I've had," I say. While writing eight hundred words on a water-tasting competition pays the bills, it's not a subject that inspires great intellectual engagement. It's also really hard to find synonyms for water that don't sound stupid. You can only say "the wet stuff" so many times before you start to question your own sanity.

"The one I got right before my book deal was 'seven hundred fifty words on prenatal yoga but try not to make it too yoga.' I was like, too yoga? Try not to make the yoga piece too yoga? I knew that I could write and make money, but I didn't like my topics," Stephanie says. She dabbled with essays on a knitting email list, some of which made it into her first book. But it took SARS, an international public health crisis, to force her to publish her work in a larger forum. Because of it, Stephanie, a lactation consultant and a doula, and her now husband Joe lost their jobs in the span of two weeks.

"You can plan for one person losing a job, but two? It happened too fast," she says.

"I remember looking up at the ceiling and thinking, 'Okay. There has got to be something you can do to get yourself out of this. Think. What are you good at? I'm like okay . . . I'm good at writing and I'm good at knitting.' And my next thought was 'Shit. This is never going to work.'"

Rather than sink into abject despair, Stephanie did what any sensible knitter would do when faced with a project that "fetched her not." She stuffed it into a closet and cast on something new.

"I got up the next day and wrote a letter to Linda Roghaar, my agent, and said, 'I think I can write a funny knitting book.' She said, 'Maybe. We'll see.' She'd never raise your hopes of selling a book if they shouldn't be raised. Really, at the time when the first book came out, I don't think anyone was ready for knitting humor. Like, knitting humor? What kind of stupid genre is that?"

It took a lot of convincing to get a publisher to bite on the idea. Cracking wise about a craft that was commonly perceived as the purview of little old ladies didn't seem like a hot seller.

"There really wasn't anybody doing it. We didn't know if it would work. So we started shopping a book of essays at the same time I started the blog. I know a lot of people think that I got my book deals because of my blog, but the timing on it is all wrong. People kept turning down the book of essays. Storey Publishing came back to me and said, 'We don't want a book of knitting essays because that could never work, but we think that there could be lighter, less complex knitting writing. Bite-sized things about knitting. That could be funny,'" Stephanie says.

"They felt more or less like knitting didn't have enough gravitas to support whole essays. Mark Twain wrote essays about erasers. It is not your topic."

Stephanie, who has since gone on to be called the Erma Bombeck of the knitting world, points out that it's not the topic that makes the work funny but the writer.

"Erma Bombeck wrote about housework. Housework is not funny. Erma Bombeck wrote about the suburbs. The suburbs are not funny. The Three Stooges slipped on banana peels. Banana peels are not funny. Cream pies are not funny—until someone catches one in the face. Then it's a riot."

Stephanie agreed to write *At Knit's End: Meditations for Women Who Knit Too Much* for Storey. Then, within days, she sold her essay book, *Yarn Harlot: The Secret Life of a Knitter*, to publisher Andrews McMeel. "Then I sort of got shafted into writing two books in a year, which I don't recommend. Something in you dies when you do that," Stephanie says, laughing.

"When you were lying in bed, wondering how it would all work out, did you expect it to get as big as it has?" I ask.

"No! How could you possibly?" Stephanie says. "I mean, Yarn Harlot won best Canadian blog this year. The blogging community in Canada shattered into a million pieces, lay on the floor, and sobbed. Because they could not believe that knitting had anything to do with the wildly gripping field of blogging. They couldn't believe it. They were like, 'Where did this come from?' I feel like sending them sympathy cards saying, 'I don't know. Dude, I'm writing about buttons. I'm sorry. I agree. The prime minister is more important.' People say that to me all the time: 'Did you ever think this would happen?' How could this happen to anybody? How could writing funny things about knitting be anybody's job?"

"Would you like to write funny things about other things?" I ask.

"I do. Nobody has noticed. If you look at the blog, there's lots of things on there that are about other things," Stephanie says.

Like "One Little Sock," which is in *Yarn Harlot: The Secret Life of a Knitter*, her first book of essays. Back in Stephanie's doula days, she used to knit during a client's labor. She'd start a baby sock when she arrived. If she finished that before the birth, she'd start another. If that got done, a hat. If the labor went on, she'd cast on increasingly larger items. "Not the afghan!" all her clients would plead, laughing. Most of the time, all that was finished by the time the baby made his or her grand entrance was a pair of socks.

But with one birth, all she had time for was one little sock, which would never be worn by the baby who didn't survive. It's a heartbreaking story and one that is only marginally about yarn. Instead, it's a story about grief that just happens to have knitting in it. "One Little Sock" also makes me cry each time I read it.

"If you don't write about the full depth of things . . . Jokes don't mean anything if you're not breaking somebody's heart a few pages later. You need the contrast," Stephanie says. "The real secret is that I have never, ever, ever written about knitting. I've only ever written about knitters, who are just people. That leaves the whole thing wide open. I'm getting away with murder, really."

"So did Mark Twain," I point out. "He wasn't writing about erasers."

"He got away with murder too," Stephanie says.

I then wander off on my own gripe about knitting humor as a genre that is the Rodney Dangerfield of the book world. Via a strange set of circumstances, I wound up exchanging emails with an editor of the *New York Times Book Review* around the time of the Yarn Harlot's Represent Tour, when Stephanie was booked at FIT. I pitched a story about it to said editor.

The response came quickly, which was (and I'm paraphrasing), "Sweetie, it's about knitting." The subtext was clear: why would any august publication waste its time writing about such a pedestrian, old ladyish subject?

I then wanted to fire back with an email asking why any august publication would waste its space writing about yet another novel in which a white college professor sleeps with a much younger student to get over a midlife crisis. Fortunately, I didn't hit send, but it was a near thing.

We are distracted at this point by the dessert menu. Even just dreaming about a nice crème brûlée takes the edge off our ire.

"I'm knitting an Alice Starmore sweater," I say. "Her stance seems to be that if you don't knit it exactly as spec'd, you have done something tragic and incorrect. My question is, am I still knitting an Alice Starmore sweater even if it's not exact?"

"Do you think you are?" Stephanie asks.

"I don't want to influence your answer," I respond.

"But your answer is my answer," she says. "I think it's all about your perception. Knitting is a self-generated activity. You can't be knitting and have anybody else have anything to do with it at the same time. It's incompatible. It's something that only you can do. It's a one-person activity. Alice Starmore has nothing to do with it. Knitters say things like, 'The pattern's a Teva Durham. I changed the neck. I made the arms shorter. I put a vent in the back and I added pleats. She's a *great* designer,'" Stephanie says, laughing. " 'But I'm still totally giving her credit even though at that point it doesn't have anything to do with her anymore.'

"It's like the argument, 'Is knitting art or is knitting craft?' For me, it's the same terrible, wishy-washy answer. It's both. It depends on how you're doing it. If you buy a pattern and buy the yarn the pattern suggests and knit it in the color suggested, you're executing someone else's directions, no matter how much joy you do it with; that's craft. That's execution. The definition of art for human beings is that it is self-expression. So the minute that you say, 'I think this would be better in pink,' or the minute that you say, 'I think the sleeves should be a little bit shorter,' the minute that who you are begins to influence what that thing is, now it's art. So I think what you have to ask yourself is that as long as you are executing what Alice intends for you, you're knitting an Alice Starmore sweater. The minute you say, 'I think the sleeves should be a little bit shorter,' or 'I think it should be this color green,' at that point maybe you're knitting almost-an-Alice, an Alice Starmore–inspired sweater.

"I don't think there's a definition, like, you've changed two things, so now it's not an Alice Starmore anymore. Or if you change all of the colors, is it an Alice Starmore? I think it's all in your perception. If you feel that there's been enough of a departure, that now it's more about you than her, then you're not anymore. I think it's all about how much of you comes to play in it."

"I think that I am knitting something very, very close to what she had in mind. Is it exact? No," I say.

"But there's that whole thing, right? An *Alice Starmore*."

"That's why the question becomes important. Because if it were like one of Ann Budd's sweater formulas in another color, I wouldn't think twice about it," I say. Budd's pattern books distilled the basic math of sweaters into easy-to-follow charts. She has done the calculations for both sizes and yarn weights. Once you've knit a swatch out of your chosen fiber, you can plug the number of stitches you get per inch into your chart and knit a basic pullover or cardigan.

I'm also, additionally, inept at following Budd's formulas. The first pair of socks I ever made was her design. Because I can't always add reliably, the finished socks didn't fit my big feet. I spent a month asking everyone I knew what their shoe size was, like some sort of reverse Goldilocks. Eventually, the socks found a home with a short friend of mine. She assures me that even in Texas, she occasionally wears wool socks. It's sweet of her to lie.

"It's interesting because the answer to 'Do you think you're knitting a Starmore?' is going to be different for everybody," Stephanie says. "I saw an Alice Starmore online, one of her cable ones, knit out of—just hold on to something to steady yourself—Red Heart acrylic yarn in the Fiesta colorway. It was rainbow variegated. It was blinding. I bet when Alice Starmore saw that, it was so far from her vision that she was like, 'Please do not call this an Alice Starmore. That is clearly your interpretation.' But she wrote the pattern. They are all her cables. And that person could say that they had not departed at all," Stephanie says.

An image pops into my mind. A Ravelry knitter used the Mary Tudor pattern but used sixteen colors (all blues, greens, yellows, and grays) instead of eleven. This knitter also changed the button bands and collar. The result captures almost none of the joyful exuberance of Starmore's design but contains recognizably the same images. I can clearly say that that represents a not-a-Starmore-anymore. But how close to that example does my sweater lie?

"Sometimes I have bad, dirty feelings if I use, like, a pattern distributed by Berroco and not Berroco yarn. I feel I've violated something sacred," Stephanie says. "The artist's vision, you know. I've compromised the integrity of what they had planned for the world. I probably only feel that way because I've seen a couple of my patterns knit in ways that I had never imagined and thought, *'This is not my vision.'*

"At that point I remember what my mother used to say to me, which is that one of the central tenets of a happy person is that when they give something away, they cease to care what happens to it," Stephanie says. "I struggle with that."

During the drive back home, I decide to teach Maddy how to knit. Given how many of the fine knitters I've met learned when they were kids, it is past time for me to teach my firstborn the craft. She's almost seven, which, compared to Stephanie learning at age four, seems like a ripe old age to learn.

And this way, she can knit her own winter hat.

When it comes to other people's kids, I am a very patient woman. Ask me to teach your child how to tie his shoes and I'll sit with him for the better part of an hour, laces in hand. Ditto writing his name or folding his shirts. I'm all over it.

As a further demonstration of my vast wells of patience, I spend my days teaching other people's kids—albeit older kids—how to speak in public or report a story. I can come up with a gazillion different ways to explain something, if it helps, and will answer any question, no matter how silly. Sometimes I even do it with a tiny, beatific smile playing on my lips.

Ask me to do the same for my own children and the results will be different. And by "different," I mean the exact opposite. If my offspring don't pick up any skill that I'm trying to teach them in less time than it takes to read this sentence, there will be sulking. And by "sulking," I'm referring to myself.

It has always been like this. Somehow, my brain has decided that the children that I gave birth to should be able to do whatever I can do, as if learned skills can cross the placental barrier. Maddy, my subconscious seems to rationalize, has my eyes; therefore she also has my ability to ride a bike or peel potatoes. And because I seem to think she can already do something because I can do it, I get really irritated when she can't pick it up instantaneously.

I have taught at least a dozen people to knit over the years. My reason for teaching them was selfish; I didn't want to knit alone. None of these people later needed therapy. Or, if they did, it had nothing to do with my teaching them how to knit. The same may not be true for my firstborn.

She and I went downtown to the yarn shop and picked up some soft pink yarn that would be perfect for a small swatch, because she should learn to accept them early. When we got home, I cast on and demonstrated the basics of the knit stitch.

She let me get about halfway through my demo before wandering off to get something to drink.

"Mad," I said, "do you really want to learn this?"

"Yes, Mom," she said. She jumped back up on the couch next to me.

"So you put the needle through the stitch, like this," I said, in my most patient voice.

"Can I have a snack?" she said, fiddling with the cuff of her shirt.

"I thought you wanted to learn how to knit."

"I do. But I'm *sooo* hungry."

"Let's just get through this first . . . Would you stop teasing Barney with the ball of yarn that I'm trying to knit with?"

"Sorry."

"So you put the needle through the . . . What are you doing?"

"Nothing."

"Nothing? You expect me to believe that turning on the TV and flipping around for *WordGirl* is nothing?"

"I do it all the time," she said. "What's the big—"

"Do you want to learn this or not?"

"I can do both. I can watch TV and you at the same time."

"I don't think you can," I said, because she can't.

"I can."

"Turn off the TV."

"Okay," she said, turning off the TV. "Now can I have a snack?"

It is at this point that I think about rapping her firmly across the knuckles with the knitting needles.

"Don't. You. Want. To. Learn. This?"

"If I learn it, can I have an apple? With peanut butter?"

"You just had lunch. Besides, now you are learning how to knit."

"Can I eat my apple and knit?"

"Why do I even bother making lunch? You don't eat it, then go scrounging for a snack. Lunches don't just spring out of nowhere, you know. There are starving kids who . . . What are you doing?"

"Waiting."

"For what?"

"For you to teach me how to knit."

We look at each other for a moment. Her expression makes it clear that she expects me to deliver knowledge to her, like gossamer from an angel's wings. My expression makes it clear that if she doesn't sit her rear in one place and listen, there will be consequences.

"You have to sit still," I said. "Can you do that?"

"That's what I've been doing," she said, "while waiting for you to teach me."

"No, you haven't," I said.

"Yes, I have."

"No, you haven't . . . Where are you going now?"

"I'm getting my library book. Knitting is boring."

I can't help but wonder where I failed as a mother.

8

NOVEMBER

Cutting a Steek

Weekend at Knitter's Review Retreat: $380

There comes a time in every Fair Isle knitter's life when she must suck it up and steek. That time, my friends, is upon us.

Steeks are just one of the Shetland knitters' contributions to the craft. When you are knitting a sweater per week so that you can pay the bills, some efficiencies must be undertaken. These knitters crafted their garments as tubes, with extra stitches placed where the sleeves will go and, in the case of a cardigan, where the front opening will be. When the shoulders of the tube are grafted shut, with Kitchener stitch in my case, the knitter cuts through the center of the armhole stitches and starts a sleeve.

Most sensible knitters blanch at the thought of very sharp things getting anywhere near their work. When you can undo hours and hours of knitting by just pulling on one thread, the idea of deliberately cutting into your laboriously crafted fabric is crazy talk. Yet I'm about to do it. But I don't want to do it alone.

So far, Lana's body has taken me the better part of nine months. I haven't worked on it without interruption. I've slept, for one. I've worked at my real job. I've minded children, attended swimming lessons (where I've discovered that I can't work on Lana poolside because the moist, warm air makes the wool into felt as I'm working it), and read bedtime stories. I've even worked on other knitting projects, small ones.

Lana has not been the sole focus of my life. If you boiled down all the time I've spent knitting the body, it would add up to four weeks of unbroken work. I'd starve if it were my only source of income, but given the mayhem of the rest of my life, I feel I've done well. Once I get the steeks cut, all that will be left are sleeves. How long can sleeves take?

On the great knitting speed continuum, with making one dishrag per year as the bottom of the scale, I fall somewhere in the middling progress to downright zippy range. Compared to some knitters, whose mental health I question, I am a mere dilettante.

"The busy hands of industrious knitter Jane Alencewiz, of Colonia, New Jersey," writes Macdonald in *No Idle Hands*, "produced within a recent six-month period a quantity to match the output of an eighteenth-century worker: three sleeveless vests, a long-sleeved turtleneck sweater, two dozen miniature sweaters as Christmas decorations, fifteen ascot scarves, two feather-and-fan afghans as wedding gifts, plus two large crocheted afghans for bridal shower gifts, a dozen pairs of slippers in assorted sizes, eight Christmas tree potholders and a piece-quilted double bed quilt as an ordination gift for her priest and a crib-sized quilt."

I marvel much at Alencewiz's devotion to the craft and hope that the crib-sized quilt was not also for her priest.

All throughout the knitting of my sweater tube, which is now sewn shut at the top, which makes it more like a sweater envelope and even more impractical for wear by human beings with heads and arms, I've been dreading the moment when I had to bust out the scissors. So I did what any right-thinking knitter would do, I took Lana with me to a knitter's retreat. If nothing else, my anxiety would be spread out among many. But if I was very, very lucky, someone there will have done this before and can hold my hand.

This is my approach to all stressful life events. Find someone who has been through childbirth, mortgage refinancing, and/or potty training and cling to her like a kindergartener on her first day of school.

The Knitter's Review Retreat was started in 2002 by Clara Parkes, editrix extraordinaire. Parkes's *Knitter's Review* website, which premiered two years earlier, is the go-to place for accurate yarn reviews, where she treats every skein that tickles her to a full workout that includes blind swatch knitting and hard-core abrasion tests. *Knitter's Review* also tackles books and tools in *Consumer Reports*–style write-ups. But for a really excellent time, you have to hit the forums.

If the yarn world could be said to have its own *Top Gear* guys, both of them would be Parkes. Her *Knitter's Book of*

Yarn strips down everything one could ever want to know about how any chosen fiber is made. Parkes can tell you, clearly, the differences between an "S-spin" and a "Z-spin" and why you should care. Her *Knitter's Book of Wool* focuses in even more sharply, detailing even the differences among the wools from different breeds of sheep.

The first Knitter's Review Retreat drew forty-nine knitters to a mountain lodge in Virginia. The 2008 retreat drew ninety-eight knitters to a prototypical New England inn in western Massachusetts in November. And I was one of those lucky ninety-eight. The retreat books up quickly enough each year that I stalked the registration page for weeks in advance, ready to pounce when the line formed. The pouncing paid off.

For me, the trip was a short one, up over the Berkshires and into Williamstown. The two-hour drive was gorgeous, if winter bleak. Bare trees stuck out of the steep hillsides like toothpicks, throwing harsh shadows in the afternoon light. Even though I left right after my one p.m. class, when I arrived it was almost dark and, to honor the language of the state, wicked cold. It's a wonder more people don't go completely bonkers during a northeastern winter. And I say this as one of the few who really like that dark and snowy season.

Inside the inn, knitters lounged on every flat surface, from the floor to the sofas to leaning against walls, knitting. I ponder, briefly, what the other guests in the inn think about this occurrence. There's also a convention of fire chiefs around on the first night. On Sunday, a flock of clergy. It's hard to say how many of them were cornered by an eager knitter and forced to learn the basics.

Near the door, one woman—only a single knitting male was in our knitterly ranks—had the good sense to bring a hiker's headlamp so that she could keep a sharper eye on her work. This genius stroke was mitigated by how fiercely others were blinded whenever she looked up, but every great idea has some bugs to be worked out.

I knew no one in the room. Participants ranged in age from just out of college to just sent grandchild off to college. The mix was relatively diverse in race and socioeconomic status. Some knitters save all year for this retreat; others don't blink at the cost. I had time to think these thoughts because I was afraid to walk into the lobby, which is where everyone gathered before the dining room opened.

I'd like to say that I am gregarious and outgoing in any situation. I'd also like to say that I look exactly like Heidi Klum. But in new situations, I tend to cling to the wall and observe. Knitters—or, at least, these knitters—won't let you do that. My roomie, Meg, who'd been to the retreat for a couple of years running, pulled me over and introduced me to the folks she was sitting with.

Even in a situation full of other lovers of knitting, I have a knack for saying the wrong thing. A few weeks earlier, I'd seriously put my foot in a big pile of stink by mentioning to my Tuesday night knitting group that the election was coming up and we would need to cancel our meeting because we'd all be home watching to see who would win: Obama or McCain. This touched off a comment about who one knitter hoped would win. Once the dust settled, we all had to agree to disagree.

In a roomful of women (and one man) who are knitting, I learned that the best thing to do is pull a completed-but-for-sleeves Mary Tudor out of your bag. Conversation will naturally follow. Most of it will make you feel like a goddess, even if you do keep explaining that it isn't as tricky as it looks.

After a New England boiled dinner of beef, carrots, parsnips, and potatoes, we adjourn to a meeting room to sit in a big circle and have show-and-tell. Clara, whose enthusiasm and snark meet in a wholly engaging way, instructs us to state our knitting philosophy while we hold up our item. It is a little like AA, like we should start every explanation with "My name is Adrienne and I am a knitter." Of course, the rejoinder will be "Hi, Adrienne!"

I make a mental note to start doing this every time I meet someone new, even if I know she doesn't knit. *Especially* if I know she doesn't knit, because how amusing will it be to see her response? Thoughts like this may be why I'm crap at parties.

I hold up Lana. There are gasps. No, really. Actual gasps. I stick my hands up into the shoulder corners and say, "My name is Adrienne and I appear to have knitted a very complicated pillowcase."

My knitting philosophy is fairly easy to explain, since it is only five words: How hard could it be? I also explain that Lana represents something larger, my quest to find out what makes knitters knit when there are so many other ways to spend their time and money. Lastly, I shamelessly beg—not for folks to buy the book, although that would be nice too, but for someone to hold my hand while I perform my armhole surgery. There are a few volunteers. Plans are made.

You'd think that there can't be more than a couple of knitting philosophies, but as we go around the circle, a couple of themes emerge. Perhaps the most popular is a variation on "I knit so that I don't kill anyone," the repetitiveness of knitting as a balm for life's aches and pains. Julia Child is quoted, at least once. "Find something you're passionate about," she said, "and keep tremendously interested in it."

But there are others, each more interesting than the last. One knitter held up a blanket her husband had accidentally felted in the wash. To her, this was the physical embodiment of making the best of things that life hands you. Another woman cited her belief that no life event should pass without a knitted item. A woman who knits to make memories had just knitted one hundred yarmulkes for her grandson's bar mitzvah. For every knitter, a slightly different story.

Which isn't to get all encounter-groupy and sappy. There is heckling. There are opinions. There are a few projects that are, to put it mildly, not to my taste. But the ultimate message seems to be, "Even if I can't stand to look at your knitting, I will defend your right to knit it." Which is fair enough.

I wander up to bed shortly after the two-hour show-and-tell ends because I'm feeling a little peaky. By morning, I feel worse and wonder if I'm spreading the plague to my knitting sistren (and one brother). Ultimately, this feeling will turn into bronchitis, probably given to me by one of my beloved offspring, who can't share their toys but can share their germs. I sniffle and hack through most of the rest of the weekend.

After a leisurely breakfast, where I drink more cups of coffee than one ought to, it's off to class. This retreat offers three options: Kathryn Alexander's knitted doodads (her word), Shelia January's hand coverings, and Melissa Morgan Oakes's two socks on two circular needles. For the hand coverings class, I pull out the homework—a, sigh, swatch—that I'd completed before I left home.

Three hours later—and after a break for doughnuts—I have one mitten finished. (This mitten, sadly, will be destroyed by Barney hours after I walk in my back door. Because it said mean things about his mama, that's why. Or so I interpret from the look he gives me as I shake the now thumbless and damp mitten in his furry face.)

It's a fine class. My socks, which were knitted one at a time on double-pointed needles, are still on. But I'm really not at the retreat for a class. Nor am I there for the shopping, which starts after lunch in the inn's basement. That doesn't stop me from buying yarn from String Theory, the yarn shop near Clara's house in Blue Hill, Maine. Some love just takes you buy surprise, which is why I can't resist a chartreuse wool/silk blend that is thousands of miles from a color I'd normally pick.

Initially I blame my nascent fever. I still love the yarn, lo these many months later. So my illness is irrelevant. It does force me to take a nap, however, which just makes me mad because I feel like I'm missing out on all the fun. I can hear knitters woo-hooing even as I shut my eyes.

The real adventure comes after a dinner of turkey with stuffing and mashed potatoes—you can say what you'd like about a retreat devoted to knitting, but you can't argue with the food—when I corner Anjeanette Milner. "The falcon howls at midnight," I say, then tip my fedora. She nods, knowingly, sniffing the white carnation in her lapel. Actually, what I say is "I'm ready." She still nodded knowingly, sans flower. It is time for my knitter's bris.

Anj, who'd gotten married to her partner, Sue, the month before the retreat and is still glowing a bit from the event, has sharp scissors and knows how to use them. Before Williamstown, I knew her in the way that you can know anyone online, which is to say that I knew the basic outlines of her life but had no idea what she looked like. She'd been following the progress of Lana on my blog. A few days before the retreat, we both figured out that we'd be there. Anj, who lives in Philadelphia, promised to hold my hand during the first cut.

The knitters take over the hotel's big meeting room on Saturday night. Some of the knitters who had brought spinning wheels proceed to make their own yarn. Most have brought projects. The one man brought his extra-large ball winder—I'll let you insert your own pun here—and we converted our hanks of yarn into convenient center-pull balls. Anj and I flop down onto the floor, which is carpeted in a baroque, black and pastel floral short pile. I pull Lana out of her bag and hand her to Anj. Surgeonlike, she hands the scissors to me handles first and smooths out the armhole line so that I know exactly where to go.

We've not attracted much of a crowd, which is good, because some things are best done in private your first time. Most knitters who are wise in the ways of the steek advise having one stiff drink before cutting in order to settle your nerves. These same knitters warn that two drinks is a bad idea, because that is when you get careless. Three drinks is right out. Given how hopped up I am on decongestants, I have no drinks. I do a couple of *ujjiya* breaths, which have been a lingering gift from my former yoga instructor, and feel okay. I cut. Three seconds later, it's done.

"That's it?" I ask.

"That's it," Anj says.

Nothing unravels. Lana remains herself, only now there is an opening, around which I'll pick up stitches (using a knitting needle to pull a strand of yarn through stitches) at the edge of the armhole, then knit a sleeve from the shoulder down. But I won't do that tonight. Picking up stitches requires counting; counting requires a quiet room with no distractions. The room that I am in is full of like-minded women making joyful noises. And I'd like to join them.

The next morning, we reconvene. Before we all scatter back across the countryside and into our regular lives, Clara, who is wearing a queenly tiara, has two things planned. First, we are to write our goals—either knitting or larger life-related—on a sheet of paper, which will be sealed in an envelope for us to read at the retreat next year. Those who did this last year get their previous letters back before writing the next one.

I write "Finish the damn Starmore," seal my envelope, and place it in Clara's special box.

The last group activity is to cast on for a "new beginnings" project, one that has special meaning to us. For example, last year Anj cast on for a wedding shawl, which she wore a few short weeks ago. If we're so inclined, Clara suggests, we should have the knitters we've come to know knit a row or two on our project.

It's a heartwarming idea, one that marries the physical warmth of yarn with its emotional warmth. Sadly, I am unprepared. My hope was that I'd find something irresistible in the "stash lounge," which is where all ninety-eight knitters brought the balls from their stash that they realized they'd never use. All these castoffs are sorted by weight and composition. An entire folding table is devoted to "good old wool." If you leave a ball, you can take a ball. I was ruthless in my stash culling and left many balls. I snatched a lot of good stuff but am not ready to cast on with any of it yet.

Instead, I'm touched that so many of the women who started as strangers a few days ago want me to knit a bit on their projects. I hope their new beginnings will be all they hope.

9

December and January
The Sleeve Death March

One box of SpongeBob Band-aids: $3.27

One of the life lessons I am unable to learn is that sleeves leach away your will to live.

They seem like such a promising phase of sweater knitting. You *only* have sleeves left to do. But there are two of them. They are long. They require shaping, so you have to pay attention to which row you're on so that you don't wind up with all the decrease bunched down at the wrist. As much as I love a good leg-of-mutton sleeve, which is tight up to the elbow, then explodes at the upper arm, it isn't the look Alice was going for. Nor is it a good look for someone with linebacker shoulders, which I have in spades.

Time is ticking by quickly. By the time I get started on sleeve number one, it's already January, even though I cut the steek at the end of November. Yes, I got a little distracted during the holiday season, which just gets longer every silly year. I also spent a lot of December curled up in a ball on my bed wondering how I would finish both the sweater and the manuscript by March first. I find acute anxiety to be a great motivator, once I get past the fear and denial stage.

Once I put my head down and knit, you'd think the sleeves would be over more quickly than a socialite's singing career. They are not. I start to develop a blister—more of an abrasion, really—across the top of the ring finger on my right hand from where the yarn rubs as I tension it. Apparently, I am a delicate flower who can't knit for hours on end without injury. The computer mouse–related pains in my right index finger raise their worrying little heads too, and the race is on to see which part of my body will crap out first.

I've managed to stay injury-free during the body of Mary Tudor because I'm lazy and spread the work out over five months. Now that the deadline is creeping ever closer, I'm knitting during every free moment. Maddy, still hatless, consents to leave me to my work. I try to enlist her to keep her ever-curious three-year-old brother away from My Precious, but she is a poor guard dog who is distracted by cartoons. I've taken to sitting in an upholstered armchair that is backed up against a wall in the living room so that I can see him coming from all sides. I know the pattern well enough to pick it back up after I've been jumped on, but this position gives me enough warning to scrunch my stitches down on the needle so that they don't fall off when he pounces.

The only bandages I can find in the house for my blister have SpongeBob characters on them, which I wear constantly for the next few weeks. One of my college students asks me in the middle of class, "Who lives in a pineapple under the sea?" It takes me a while to figure out what she's talking about.

Alice Starmore seems to be tentatively stepping back into the knitting world. She revved up her Virtual Yarns site in 2001, not long after the contretemps with Broad Bay. For it, she developed her own line of yarn, which she sells online both as single skeins and in kits. Some of the kits include patterns; some don't. For example, with the Tudor Roses sweaters, you can buy a yarn pack for Henry VII, Anne of Cleves, Elizabeth I, Margaret Tudor, and Catherine Parr. Elizabeth I is knitted straight from the book; the others come with enhanced schematics and in a broader range of sizes.

There are new-to-me designs as well, most from books I don't own, each more gorgeous than the last. And their price is dear, running in the hundreds of dollars for both yarn and pattern. Would I be as enamored with them if I could pick them up at a big box craft shop like A. C. Moore or Michaels? Is it their relative scarcity that sucks me in?

I honestly don't know. I'd like to think that I'm not that shallow but evidence points elsewhere. Back in the early nineties, I was a huge fan of the J. Peterman catalog, not because I loved the clothes but because I loved the story behind them. In the back of my brain, I knew that the copy was turned out by some dude at a desk who made up quite a bit of it out of whole cloth, pun intended. Despite the fact that I couldn't afford to buy anything, since I was in college, I aspired to buy something from J. Peterman one day soon.

I'm surprised that the catalog still exists, frankly, just because both the prices and the concept are outrageous. Perhaps the *Seinfeld* character kept the J. Peterman myth alive. A sample from the online version, about a rose-patterned shirt ($119):

> Ruddigore Hall's 400-year-old facade has received a steam facial for the wedding of the social season.
>
> In the portrait gallery, Pimm's Cups are served with odd little canapés of smoked venison and bits of quince. Tweedy toffs debate the fillies running at Newmarket, while the Sloanies attending a nearby cooking school are dissected by the women, all wearing fanciful hats . . . all except you, of course.
>
> "Roses don't do well in the shade," you tell a heavy-breathing baronet who appears fascinated by the lush hybrids on your blouse.
>
> "Old French Roses, I believe," a plummy voice interrupts. "Grow them myself." It's Lord Randolph to your rescue, but not for long; Lady Margaret has you both now well within her sights.
>
> You must expect such things to happen when you upstage the bride.

The evocative copy of Starmore's Virtual Yarns site also taps that same impulse, the desire for a product that represents more than a mere sweater pattern or simple skein of yarn. In the early part of the millennium, Alice developed her own range of yarns based on the flora, fauna, and views of Isle of

Lewis, where she and countless generations of her clan now live. Virtual Yarns may be the J. Peterman of the wool world, except I think that Starmore is sincere.

Alice lambasted Rowan on her site when the company made Lewis and Harris, the source of Harris tweed, the same island in some advertising copy about a new line of yarns:

"I had a look and found the text arresting, to say the least, for it appeared that the identity of myself, and my forefathers for centuries back, had been changed overnight by the Rowan yarn brand," Alice writes. "Rowan's piece extolled the virtues of Harris Tweed, which they said was produced *'on a small island in the Outer Hebrides, Scotland—the island of Lewis, also known as Harris.'*

"How do I explain the sheer, staggering volume of ignorance embedded within those few words? Let me try. Imagine if, when writing about the north of England, I blithely stated, 'Yorkshire, also known as Lancashire.' If I wrote that then I would be metaphorically tarred and feathered—perhaps even literally too. And rightly so."

Confusing the names of the Hebridean Isles is a source of scorn to Alice, but if you need a lesson in sarcasm and bile, you should take a minute and read her discussion of the Insolvency Report she received from Rowan's lawyer.

So that she has plenty of ammunition when she fires back at me, I live in Oneonta, which shouldn't be confused with Upstate New York, nor should it be called Downstate. We are in the Southern Tier, if you want to get technical, and have our own rich history that involves trains, hops production, colleges, and minor league baseball. The folks who settled here wiped out the Iroquois, not the Algonquins, and were Dutch/German more than British. We have the best New York–style pizza one can get outside Manhattan and the other four boroughs. If you go to Alfresco's, ask for the "cold cheese" slice, which is a delicacy that you will find nowhere else. If you get any of this wrong, or confuse us with Altoona (or, worse yet, the Oneonta in Alabama), then you've neglected our rich heritage and ought to be tarred and feathered.

You can see how silly this can get and how quickly.

I understand the temptation to pick apart every last utterance by someone you perceive as an enemy. I understand that Alice has been done wrong. I understand how much that hurts and how much she wants to strike back. I'd lay even money that everyone gets this impulse, not just me.

Wound licking is a necessary part of the healing process, but eventually, you need to get past it. And I'm not just talking about Alice here. My country spent eight long years on the wrong end of a pointy stick. We are bitter too, and not just a little bit hurt. Yet we're trying to let bygones be just that in order to get the work done, to slap a few SpongeBob Band-aids on the worst of the wounds so that we can keep doing what we're best at, which is getting shit done.

There are some, of course, who think that I and others like me are liberal pinko whiny-ass crybabies who didn't appreciate the great mind of George W. Bush. To them, those eight years were the best years ever. Those folks are welcome to their opinions, even if I don't want to have a beer with them. As long as you don't expect me to wear it, I will support your right to knit what you want, no matter how hideous I think the end result will be.

I want Alice to move past this and start getting shit out because, if nothing else, her shit is gorgeous. The amount of thought and care that she puts into her work inspires awe. Like her new line of yarn that the Virtual Yarns site sells. Even if the essays about her thought process are crafted to play up the rarity of her product, the product itself remains divine—unlike J. Peterman's clothes, which, when I finally bought something, turned out to just be clothes. Nice clothes, mind, but I didn't suddenly find myself drinking Pimm's Cups at a garden wedding.

Online, Starmore exquisitely details each thought that went into her Hebridean yarn's production. The line is divided into four color families: Moor and Mountain, Sea and Shoreline, Birds, and Summer Isle. Alice would go on long walks where she'd collect, magpielike, the bits of nature that caught her eye. The colors in each range could not be more perfect representations of her home.

She documents her thought process too, explaining that some of the colors, like Summertide, were based not on a specific object but on a feeling. But most of her hues were born from what she saw, if highly refined. There are plants, like Whin and Witchflower, whose weedy essence illuminates the yarn. Each of the bird yarns—from Solan Goose to Kittiwake—captures each species' personality and tones.

Her descriptions read like postcards, simultaneously romanticizing her home, which is a place most won't know as intimately as she does, and humanizing it. She tells stories about young men poaching salmon, about the selkie and the kelpie stealing souls, about inlets rippling pure blue.

For those who are taken with such rich history, both the yarn and the yarns about it snuggle into your sweet spot and don't let go.

Until late 2008, Starmore's work sat neglected. The patterns and kits sold enough, I guess, to keep paying the site's hosting fees. But a few months ago, Alice started to drip back into the knitting public's consciousness. Word leaked out that her *Book of Fair Isle Knitting* would be reprinted in August 2009. Then Starmore also released her new book, *Road Movies, Volume 1,* which features zero patterns, is self-published, and is available only from her website. *Road Movies* is a diary, of sorts, about a series of road trips across the United States she took at the end of the nineties while still on the teaching and lecture circuit.

Movies moves Alice in my mind from a grumpy harridan who interacts with the larger world only long enough to grouse about it, to a free-spirited if temperamental artist who can't help drawing inspiration from what she sees and feels. I still don't feel like I know her in any meaningful way, nor am I certain that I want to. Her unflagging self-confidence gets under my skin, because it starts to edge into hubris. The single time she records feeling the smallest tinge of anxiety is just before a speech at the Smithsonian:

"I never suffer from pre-event nerves," Starmore writes. "I know my subject better than anyone else and can extemporize for as long as necessary. I am also highly experienced at what I do, and have a well-honed ability to judge an audience and tailor my delivery to suit the occasion . . . That is why I was surprised when my tummy did a loop the loop as I walked up to the lectern and surveyed the audience. I silently thought, oh bugger!"

She prevails, of course, because that is what she does. A few humanizing details slip in, like her love of Manolo Blahniks, which she wears with "a blue woolen miniskirt and matching tunic, both of which I had made myself. I knew that nobody would have seen anything quite like it." In Vegas, she masters the art of Skee-Ball (because she alone knows its secret) and gives her prize, a big stuffed bear, to the young girl nearby.

She even takes my country to task for its treatment of gay men in the early nineties: "I knew from previous visits that New York City had a large contingent of street people, but I had noticed a new group. They were men aged somewhere in their twenties and thirties, begging on the streets in the SoHo and Greenwich Village areas . . . you saw them every fifty yards or so, and each one looked really ill. In fact, their skin showed lesions and blotches and it looked as if they were dying. . . . I knew U.S. citizens took pride in the principle that there was no free lunch, but I didn't see the need to be so dogmatic about it—certainly not to the extent that Third World scenes were played out on the city streets. I never gave voice to my opinions however, and always made it a point of principle to be just 'a chield amang you taking notes.'"

For every passage that is a burr in my underpants and that demonstrates a significant lack of self-awareness, there is one that rubs lotion on the rash. "I was on a commuter train coming in from Croton-on-Hudson," Alice writes, "listening enthralled as the guard recited the names of each stop. Ossining, Tarrytown, Stuyton Duyville." I know how musical those names are because that is the exact same line I take when I head to the big city. I can instantly imagine her there, wobbling back and forth, starting at the gorgeous expanse of the Hudson River, lulled by the towns. For a moment, I know how she feels.

The irony of her misspelling of Spuyten Duyvil as "Stuyton Duyville" is not lost. Knitters in the Bronx, which is where the Duyvil is, should take their ire directly to Ms. Alice.

Or this passage, which takes place just after she checks into a hotel in Massachusetts:

> Are you blind, I thought, and indicated the lobby. "All these fellows in women's clothing."
>
> "Oh," he said, as if he'd only just noticed. "It's the convention."
>
> I was incredulous. "It's the convention in Salem on the Sabbath for men to dress up as women?"
>
> The clerk looked at me with deep sympathy, as if I had some kind of impediment, which I was indeed beginning to feel I had. "*The* convention," he repeated slowly. "They come all the way from Portland. And some from out of state."
>
> Of course! How foolish of me not to know. A drag queens' convention. A regular Oddphellows' Ball.

I can't quite escape from this need to know more about Alice, which is an impulse I have with no other designers whose work I like. I know only where they live—and have come by that information accidentally. Veronique Avery, whose elegant designs make me wish I had time to do nothing but knit, lives in Montreal. Cat Bordhi lives on an island near Seattle. *Interweave Knits* editor Eunny Jang is in greater Baltimore.

But with Starmore, my desire to understand her greatly outstrips the resources available, which may just increase my fascination. That couples with the fear that the community has of her lawyers and the response that I'd get if I showed up on her doorstep one day. Sometimes, she pushes the world away, it seems, then complains that no one understands her. She's right. We don't understand her, not really. I can barely interpret my own motivations, much less those of a near stranger. That doesn't mean, however, that I shouldn't try.

10
February
The End of the Yarn

Wooly board: $73.95 plus shipping

"Personal quests," writes Barbara Kingsolver in *Animal, Vegetable, Miracle: A Year of Food Life*, "do have a way of taking on lives of their own, even when nobody else knows or cares: recreational runners push themselves another mile, Scrabblers keep making bigger words. Our locavore project nudged us constantly toward new personal bests. But it always remains fascination, not fanaticism."

To cut directly to the chase, I finished the sweater a week before my deadline. The sleeves—oh, the stupid sleeves that make me curse my arms—took five weeks of knitting in every spare moment that I had. My summertime six weeks of no knitting put me in a bind at the very end. Holding the process back even further was the fact that the first sleeve was cursed. I picked up stitches around the armhole three times before I hit the magic number of seventy-two. I then discovered that I'd picked them all up backwards and would have to start again. I may have wept, but since no one saw me, I'll deny it.

I finished the first sleeve during the Super Bowl, nearly snapping a needle in two when it looked like my home team wouldn't prevail. When they won, I celebrated both that and binding off that last stitch.

The second sleeve, like my second kid, was easier. Not instant-pudding easy—I speak of both kid and sleeve—but easier for having done it once.

After sleeve two, I cut up the front steeks to turn my tube into a proper cardigan. I picked up stitches for a collar, knitted it, then did the same for both front button bands. I make it sound simple, I know. But once you've done it a few times, it's not difficult. It's like the difference in looking at first grade from the perspective of a kindergartener, where it seems so scary and hard, and the perspective as a fifth grader, where it seems like such a breeze compared to what you're doing now.

One of the mitered front corners is highly imperfect because I'd apparently missed a direction where I was supposed to mark a stitch back on row ten. By the time I figured out what had gone wrong—and how to make it right—I'd already finished the button band and wasn't going to rip all of it out. Alice, if she ever sees it, will have a fit. I'm cool with it, even if it does mock me every time I look at it. Flocks of Quakers (or Amish or Muslims) will fall to their knees before Lana's imperfectness.

At this point, the hardest part of finishing is tacking down the steek flaps, not because it's strictly necessary to keep them from unraveling but because it looks more finished that way. I use a simple whipstitch to connect flap to floats on the wrong side. The hard part isn't the sewing but the finishing. After coming so far and learning so much, my attention wants to stray from the simple details. But I stitch.

I'm vaguely concerned with the bag full of yarn that I have left over. Of the thirty-five skeins I ordered, thirteen are untouched. You know that sinking feeling you get when you assemble flat-pack furniture and wind up with a homeless screw? Imagine that but with a big bag of yarn.

But everything measures out. The sweater measures what the pattern says. Sleeves stay on, which is Ann Shayne's mark of sweater success. The too-much-yarn problem may just be yet another sign that simple math is my Waterloo. Regardless, I'll be knitting a lot of mittens and hats with Lana's leavings. Perhaps I'll even make the prodigal hat for my firstborn.

Apart from my previous deviations with yarn choice, I make one more now. Alice's Mary Tudor has one button up near the throat. I decide to eighty-six the button because I am a rebel. "Fuck the button," I think, flipping a mental bird to Alice as I recklessly knit on.

Actually, it's an aesthetic choice, not an attitudinal one. The sweater is busy enough without adding another ornament. I don't intend to wear it anyway.

That, my friends, is my deep, dark secret. After spending the better part of the year lugging Lana around both literally and metaphorically, I no longer want to look at it. Lately, whenever I show it to knitters, who coo and aah, I don't get their response. I toy with the idea of auctioning it off for charity or, in darker moments, stomping on it until it dissolves back into its component parts.

This is my default response to any project that I live with. The same isn't true of my children, thankfully, but that may only be because they aren't inanimate objects solely created by me. For better or worse, they have their own agency and will. Which is really irritating at times, like when one pitches a fit in the middle of the grocery store because he wants a pack of gum. But their own spirits are what will probably save them from a lifetime of therapy.

It passes, this hatred for things I make. I can look back on most of what I've written and admit that it doesn't suck as a whole, even if parts do. Eventually, the same will be true for Lana, once we get some distance from each other and can again see the beauty rather than the faults. It's like Jason, who once he survived the trials (and the really boring bits of the boat journey that the storytellers fail to mention), stuffed the Golden Fleece in a drawer because he realized that constant contact with something beautiful makes you appreciate it less. Just think of all the tragedy that could have been averted if Jason had realized that most of the fun is in the getting, not the having, then handed the Fleece off to a passing oracle.

After I made the inside seams all pretty, it was time to block Lana. In Scotland, stranded sweaters are smoothed out on a wooly board, which is a human-shaped wooden frame with removable arms that is set out in the sun while the garment dries. I also suspect the Scots soak their finished work in the nearest loch for added authenticity.

Given that I live in a loch-free neighborhood, I run to the kitchen, fill my biggest stewpot with cold water and wool wash, and chuck Lana in. While she soaks, I assemble my brand-new wooly board.

There's this great bit in Charlie Brown's Thanksgiving special—you know, the one where Snoopy and Woodstock make popcorn and toast for the day's feast—where Snoopy is wrestling with an old-fashioned wooden sling-style deck chair. The chair will have none of it and snaps the beagle's fingers, um, paws every chance it gets.

Assembling a wooly board is a lot like that. Six long pieces of lumber and three short ones keep pinching my fingers or falling on my head. My knobs won't tighten and the assembled contraption is so top-heavy it falls over if you breathe near it. I can hear generations of Scots laughing their bonny arses off at me. They may also be pointing their fingers and wetting their kilts.

I prevail, ultimately. Actually, what I do is call my very handy husband because I need a spare set of hands. He visibly restrains himself from offering advice. This is how we've managed to stay married for nearly fifteen years. I don't kibitz about his cooking; he doesn't pick at my woodworking, especially when he notices that I'm seconds away from taking a hammer to the whole silly thing while laughing maniacally. Really, a happy union may be that simple.

I pull Lana from her bath, roll her up in a couple of bath towels to squeeze out as much moisture as I can, then shrug her onto the wooly board. I pin the front closed and stand back to admire my work. Mary Tudor, as she basks in the wan early spring light, pulls my eye to her like a magnet. Totally worth every minute of sweat, blisters, and tears.

The next obstacle is sitting next to his food dish, eyeballing the distance between my sweater and his claws.

"Don't even think about it, Barney," I say.

"You have to sleep eventually," he says, with his eyes.

Hm. I'd forgotten the Barney factor. I'm not about to let this ten-pound black and white ball of muscle and fur have his way with my purty sweater.

I briefly ponder putting the wooly board and Lana outside but remember that it's all of twenty-five degrees. I need the sweater to dry, not become a sweatersicle. I briefly ponder chucking Barney outside, but no matter how tempting the idea, I realize the neighbors would call animal control. And the dogcatcher is unlikely to agree that a half-frozen cat is better than a completely shredded sweater.

Since I'm standing in the kitchen, when Barney gets close enough to sniff the hem, I spray him with water from the sink. He runs away long enough to rescrew his courage to the sticking point. He comes back in for another go. I spray him again. He runs again.

I wait, hand on sprayer.

The theme from *The Good, the Bad and the Ugly* runs through my head.

I wait a little longer.

I start to feel just a little bit silly. I also realize that I've managed to get water all over the floor.

Barney doesn't come back. I get some dishtowels and mop up.

For the next twenty-four hours—even waking out of a sound sleep a few times—I jump every time I hear the whisper of claws reaching for knitwear. Lana, somehow, dries unmolested. That alone is a miracle.

Once Lana is bone dry, I strip off the machine-made cardigan I have on and prepare for my first moments wearing her. It's here that I expect to feel rapture, when I can get away with ending this story with a "Wearing Mary Tudor: priceless" line. Damn the cliché. Here's the kicker: my sweater, which cost hundreds of both dollars and hours, doesn't fit.

The sleeves are a good six inches too short. I can't close the front over my ample bust. My linebacker shoulders stretch the collar too wide.

Here's the kicker to the kicker: I don't care.

I don't say that in a pretending-I-don't-care-when-deep-down-I-really-do-so-that-I-don't-feel-like-all-of-that-work-was-for-nothing way. I, honestly and without reservation, am untroubled by how poorly this sweater fits.

I don't know why all knitters knit. There are commonalities, sure. We knit because we need mittens. We knit because we derive pleasure from it. Mostly, we knit to manage stress, because even as the world falls around our ears, there is at least one part of our lives over which we have complete control. Unlike, say, with balky children or crashing economies, we are the gods of our own knitting. We decide how much error we are willing to live with. We decide if it lives or it dies.

Sometimes it seems that Starmore is trying to force that approach onto her interactions with other people. She tries to frog the unfroggable, to get her life's work back to its ball-of-wool state so that she can start again. But once you start dealing with other people, knitting stops working as a metaphor. Some knots can't be untied.

I don't care that my Mary Tudor doesn't fit because I didn't knit it in order to have a new sweater. I knit it because I was fascinated by it, because I thought it was a beautiful object and a challenge for my skills. Lana met those needs.

In between, I learned that I just might be a process knitter, rather than a product one. I still deeply dislike writing. But now that I have almost written this, my joy is nearly uncontainable.

If I were a fanatic about my year of knitting a Starmore, I'd rip out Lana and start one that fits, maybe using up some of my leftover balls in the process. As sick as I am of looking at Lana right this second, I can't fathom doing this. Someday I may work out the math and knit another one that is bespoke. I probably won't, however; there is just too much else to draw my fascination.

Later I may give Denny a call and see if she'll teach me to spin, just as soon as I get my hands on that Golden Fleece.

Acknowledgments

No one knits in a vacuum, if only because your yarn clogs it up.

Thanks to all the knitters who let me show up in their hometowns and pester them: Ann Shayne, Susette Newberry, Cyndi Lee, Kay Gardiner, Amy Singer, and Stephanie Pearl-McPhee. Thanks also to Rita Petteys, Jenna Wilson, Clara Parkes, Anjeanette Wilner, and all the knitters who touched Mary Tudor, either figuratively or literally.

Thanks to all my blog readers. You provide more support than you realize.

Thanks to Alice Starmore for seeing the patterns and colors that no one else had seen.

Thanks to Scott Miller, even though he never did write that knitting song for me.

Thanks to Elizabeth Kaplan and Leslie Meredith, who saw the merit in a book about a sweater.

Thanks to my Dad for the subhead and the handkerchief.

Thanks to my (mostly) patient children, Madeline and Cormac. I love you both. Equally.

Thanks to the Seeleys for keeping them occupied while I pushed through the first draft.

And, as always, all my thanks and love to my husband, Scott, who doesn't get enough praise for his seamless aid and quiet brilliance. What shall we make next?

About the Author

Adrienne Martini, a former editor for Knoxville, Tennessee's *Metro Pulse*, is an award-winning freelance writer and creative writing teacher at SUNY-Oneonta and Hartwick College. Author of *Hillbilly Gothic*, she lives in Oneonta, New York, with her husband, Scott, and children, Maddy and Cory.